Making Music

Making Music

Neville Marriner and the
Academy of St Martin in the Fields

CHRISTIAN TYLER

UNICORN PRESS

Unicorn Press
47 Earlham Road
Norwich
NR2 3AD

www.unicornpress.org

First published by Unicorn Press 2009

ISBN 978 1 906509 04 0

Designed by Mark Penfound

Printed in Slovenia for Latitide Press

Contents

by Murray Perahia, Principal Guest Conductor

My experiences with the Academy of St Martin in the Fields have all been happy ones. The players have great musical talent, skill, and goodwill, and rehearsals with them are always enjoyable. They are very dedicated musicians, completely professional but never just professional; they love to be involved, not only in phrasing the music but in every aspect of good music-making.

I wish them the very best on their 50th birthday, and many more to come.

Murray Perahia
London, October 30, 2009

THIS book is about the remarkable relationship between the Academy of St Martin in the Fields and the man who created it - probably the longest such relationship in modern musical history, and certainly one of the most productive.

The orchestra's name is a mouthful, and has caused no end of trouble in the 50 years of its existence. But thanks to the musical and business acumen of Sir Neville Marriner, the name has become familiar round the world, appearing on more recordings than that of any competitor.

The book has an evolutionary theme also. Over the years this famous group of British freelance musicians has adopted three different formats (chamber ensemble, chamber orchestra and symphony orchestra) to meet the demands of the market. Now it is having to make its way in the world without the man whose name has become so indelibly associated with it. Sir Neville, at 85, still conducts the Academy symphony orchestra; but a busy, independent career means he no longer seeks to call the tune.

I have tried not only to tell the story of the Academy's first half century, but to portray its musicians and backstage personnel and the internal dynamics which give the orchestra its unique character and sound. Concertgoers and record buyers may know a lot about classical music, but they rarely hear about the people who deliver it.

The first chapter, a description of the chamber orchestra on tour in North America, serves to introduce the musicians and some of the topics covered later. Chapter Two attempts to characterize the Academy 'sound' and the ethos that goes into making it. Chapter Three takes us back to the beginning and covers the orchestra's first decade. Chapter Four is a kind of biographical intermission, a portrait of Neville Marriner and his separate career as a conductor. The story of the orchestra resumes in Chapters Five and Six, covering the golden years of recording, the *Amadeus* film-track bonanza, followed by a brush with financial disaster, the collapse of the classical record market, and ending with the search for a new model. The end of the book is not the end of the story.

For my account of the early history of the Academy I am deeply indebted to Meirion and Susie Harries. They not only permitted me to quote freely from their book *The Academy of St Martin in the Fields* (Michael Joseph,1981), but lent me their extensive collection of notes and interviews. Philip Stuart's 1999 discography of the Academy and of Sir Neville with other orchestras ('A Record Partnership') has been absolutely invaluable. Conrad Bjørshol, of Stavanger, Norway, also saved me a great deal of labour by giving me access to his unrivalled collection of material about the orchestra and its founding director. Katy Jones was tireless in helping me sort out the Academy's domestic history, and collected the names of all those who have played for it. Sylvia Holford helped with the chorus. I wish to thank Katy, Tim Brown, and Susie Harries for reading the text in draft.

My thanks go to the many Academy musicians, past and present, who answered my questions so readily and whose names appear in the text; to friends and associates who gave me interviews; to Tara Persaud and Kay McCavic for looking after us on tour; and to the players on that tour for their delightful companionship.

I am grateful to Andrew McGee for the cartoons he drew especially for this book, and to Ciaran my wife, collaborator and counsellor for the marvellous oil sketches that adorn it.

Needless to say, the book would have got nowhere without the initial support and co-operation of Neville and Molly Marriner, who submitted to long hours of interview and read the text in draft. Their generous friendship, good humour and hospitality exemplify for me the spirit of the entire, fifty-year, enterprise.

Chapter one

ON THE ROAD

AFTER sixteen hours of travel, and a flight which has carried us a third of the way round the globe to Los Angeles, we are disgorged into a balmy Californian evening: 21 string players and their instruments, two managers from head office, and a couple of camp followers – the writer and his wife. A snow-covered England lies far behind us. Now we are thinking only of our impending tour of North America: eight cities and ten concerts in 14 days.

The band is not much larger than the original Academy of 50 years ago – seven first violins, five seconds, four violas, three cellos and two basses – and is playing, as they did, without a conductor. Instead, it will be led by Julia Fischer, the prodigious young German violinist, who will direct from the first desk of the violins when she is not playing as soloist, and stand out in front when she is.

Our first engagement is here in Costa Mesa, Orange County, one of the wealthiest places in California (and hence the world). But where are all the people? There is not a soul about. It is a Monday evening in February, the air is warm and has that Rinse-Aid sparkle which England sees only in Spring. Yet the place is deserted. From the front door of the hotel we look out across a broad campus: in front of us stands the concert hall, a large, clean-cut oblong of dazzling whiteness. There is a distant rush-hour hum from the Pacific coast freeway which we have just left, punctuated by the muffled roar of planes taking off from John Wayne airport a few miles west. If it were not for that, and the occasional car drifting past on the road outside, you would think Costa Mesa had been emptied by the plague.

The players, meanwhile, are getting straight into tour mode, checking out their rooms. A violinist, finding an ice-making machine standing sentry by her door, goes straight back to Reception to ask for a transfer.

Touring and tourism have nothing in common. For musicians on tour – as for anyone whose work takes them abroad – priorities are reversed. Tourists choose the places they visit and sights they want to see; they worry about the language, the shops, beaches and museums. For touring musicians, these things are irrelevant. The destinations have been chosen by someone else, and the journeys between them are to be endured rather than enjoyed. Where tourists like to boast how they have engaged with the locals, musicians like to travel in a bubble, a space within which they can think, practise and perform music. For them touring is no sort of holiday, except in the sense that it is a break from domestic life.

The flight had been uneventful for all but the two outsize passengers whose height and girth attract curious stares at every airport check-in. I am speaking of the double basses in their eight-foot high battered cases. They have to travel in the hold – usually with pets and other animals. Because of the extra paperwork they generate they are always the slowest members of the group. American customs officials are famously fussy and our two fat passengers were subjected to intense vetting when they came off the plane at Los Angeles. They weren't actually last out of the terminal building, however. That was us, because a sniffer dog found an apple and banana in my wife's bag, and we were sent to a special

All aboard: the first of
many bus rides.

The fattest passengers
at check-in.
Photo: Christian Tyler

food-smuggling officer for interrogation. We were lucky: later, on the bus, we
learned that on a previous tour a player had been fined $300 for importing an
alien orange, and the rest of the band clubbed together to reimburse her.

Tuesday was a day off, one of those unreal days when the jet-lagged mind
cannot quite believe it is where it is, when the body's clock has been so disrupted
that you spring awake at three in the morning, and at tea-time feel as if you
have been hit with a sandbag. Even without jet lag, Costa Mesa encourages a
sense of unreality. Some of the buildings are very fine, but the overall impression is one of sterile emptiness. The 'centre' looks like an architect's model of a
new development, blown up to gargantuan scale. Everything is at least one and a
half times bigger than in Europe, so that the people – if there were people – are
dwarfed. The first human I saw was a Hispanic woman clipping a hedge on the
path running up beside the Segerstrom Hall, a massive theatre built of red brick
in the style of ancient Samarkand facing the newer and more restrained Segerstrom Concert Hall in which the following night's concert would take place. At
the top of the path was a plinth on which reclined a bronze figure by Henry
Moore, and a few yards beyond it, another plinth supporting a red Mercedes
SLK300 sports car. The two monuments are embodiments of California: wealth,
patronage, and the automobile. A bank headquarters loomed above me, and
beyond lay the wide open spaces of downtown Costa Mesa – huge parking lots

Nigel Barratt, store manager and Leon Bosch, co-principal bass, on the way to a rehearsal in Nashville, Tennessee.

occasionally interrupted by parades of shops where restaurants and dry cleaners jostled beauty parlours with names like 'Spa and Nails' and 'The Laser Room'.

The first rehearsal of the tour was scheduled for the following morning at 11. On my way over to the hall I saw in the distance a scene that might have come from a Fellini film: passing in front of a mirrored office block which reflected the whole picture in fractured form, two small figures were wheeling the hulking double basses along a path to the stage door.

Inside, the auditorium was little short of breathtaking, like many we were to see in the coming days. An enormous space sculpted into long, flowing curves like the hull of a cruise liner, it rose five tiers above the stalls. Over the stage hung acoustic baffles of aluminium shaped like the underside of a baleen whale. The organ pipes fixed to the wall behind appeared to have been stamped out of a single metal plate. If this is how Orange County spends its money, who can begrudge it its wealth?

For this tour the Academy had brought a programme which showed off the virtuosity and musicality both of the players and of Julia, their soloist-director. At the beginng and end were two richly-scored string pieces, and in the middle – either side of the interval – Bach's two violin concertos, No.1 in A minor and No. 2 in E major. Britten's *Variations on a Theme of Frank Bridge* made a fiery opening. It is a playful, varied and difficult piece which is a favourite with the orchestra. Britten was 24 years old when he composed it for the Salzburg Festival of 1937 and dedicated it to the composer who had been his mentor. He had just a month in which to complete it. The finale was William Walton's *Sonata for Strings*, a luscious re-working of his only string quartet. Generally little known, it has strong associations for the Academy because it was the result of an approach that Neville Marriner made to the composer in 1970. Over lunch at the Ritz he asked Walton to write something for the band. Walton was disinclined – he was nearly 70 – but agreed to enlarge his 1945 string quartet in A minor. He

> Granny Denise
> +
> Grandpa Stefan
> with love from
> Tom, Jo + Kate
>
> He will be great, and called the Son
> of the Most High. Luke 1.32
>
> xxx '09
> Christmas

...nold to finish the fourth. An ...dience on one occasion when ...ement together: 'So Neville ...Walton, sitting there with his ...how laid-back Neville was.

...programme for the tour ...thought unfair on Julia, ...many pieces. The Bach ...ing them from a tender ...f them made with the ...e more or less new to ...gramme on a 12-day ...ight before. That tour ...it was the players who con-...as Julia became more familiar with the music ...role as director. 'She has nerves of steel,' one player told me. By now, the Walton had been wrapped up, and the Britten – according to Julia a more difficult piece – nearly so.

Today they start with the Bach. Harvey de Souza, leading the orchestra for the two concertos, goes to the back of the big hall to listen, returning to say that the *tuttis* sound 'great' but that the accompaniments should be more 'transparent' (a favourite musicians' term whose meaning is not itself very transparent).

A passage in one of the slow movements prompts a four-way discussion between Julia and the front desks. At another point Julia asks for more 'excitement' at which Stephen Orton, the principal cellist, makes a joke which cracks her up. While Julia is playing a long series of octave leaps over the top of the melody, Harvey asks the cellos to 'make more of a point'.

Sitting alone in the vast auditorium heightens one's attention to the music. In the opening movement of the E major I hear a beautiful counterpoint melody in the second violins and violas I have never heard before. In the slow movement, surely one of the most sublime things Bach wrote, the familiar music seems to take on a new meaning. Perhaps it's the jet lag playing tricks, but the musical dialogue sounds almost operatic: the cellos' opening phrases become a baritone, encouraging the solo violin, the soprano, to sing to him about love. She responds, shyly at first, but then with growing enthusiasm, until she can hardly stop herself singing. The players, too, seem to be savouring their own sound, like wine buffs contentedly mulling over a favourite vintage.

Such fancies apart, the interest for me was to observe how Julia Fischer, who, after all, is still only 25 years old, handled this group of older, highly accomplished and experienced players, many of whom are leaders and soloists themselves. I had watched her at a pre-tour rehearsal and concert at the Cadogan Hall off Sloane Square in London. Now, as then, I was impressed above all by her self-assurance. She knows what she wants, and how to be tactful in getting it. Her confidence comes not just from her musical ability, but from deep musicianship and a formidable memory which enables her to carry whole scores in her head. The players did not seem to mind her interventions, or occasional criticisms. Or if they did, they weren't showing it. They respect her wisdom, which is not only musical – indeed she is unnervingly mature for a 25-year-old. Onstage, her age becomes irrelevant. 'She is completely confident in her own ability and judgement, very good at the small details and with that remarkable and effort-less technique of hers, nothing flusters her,' said Pauls Ezergailis, one of the first violins. 'In a sense we make it easy for her. We present her with a more or less readymade product which she can then shape or mould. You know immediately if a musician is bluffing – she is the real thing.'

That evening, we saw the invisible citizens of Costa Mesa for the first time. From the dusky wastes of Orange County they converged in their hundreds on the lobby of the Segerstrom Hall. It was the sort of crowd you find at classical concerts everywhere: some dressed up for the occasion, most in casual clothes, and a few in outfits designed for showing off.

As the orchestra came out of the wings, I wondered how many members of the audience realised how jetlagged the players were, and I was apprehensive for them. Jetlag can play nasty tricks. Players find themselves overheating (is this something to do with the body's circadian rhythms being upset?), unable to focus, and drifting into a kind of waking sleep. On such occasions even the most confident performer can suffer a memory blank, when the mind is jolted with sudden doubt: Should I be playing now? Have I jumped ahead? Why are the first violins silent? At such times, the player has no choice but to rely on the auto-pilot, the physical memory in fingers and arms, to come safely in to land. Extra fuel seems to be injected to keep the plane aloft – a dose of adrenalin, perhaps. Performers think that audiences always notice if they are not feeling too good, but I doubt it.

Certainly, the first concert of the tour appeared to go without a hitch. After only a few bars of the Britten, the atmosphere in the great hall began to change. Supported by the collective silence, a sense of anticipation in the audience, and something like the willing suspension of disbelief that Coleridge described, the music began to drive out all other physical sensations. I felt a door shutting on the real world, and the bubble of sound created by the players gradually expanding until we were emveloped in another, warmer and more scented climate like the inside of a tropical greenhouse.[1] The skin of the bubble insulated us from the noise of the world outside, and clouded the visual impact even of the hall's flamboyant décor. Music can dissolve all our connections with the world, and the more subtle its gradations, the more demanding its internal narrative, the more complete our sense of pleasurable detachment. No wonder we resent it when the trance is broken by a barking cough or scraping chair, or by precipitate clapping the moment a piece has ended.

I noticed at this first concert, as at the rehearsal earlier, the expressiveness of Julia Fischer's body language. When leading from the first desk in performance, she sits very straight and still. In rehearsal, she might play with legs crossed, and slide down in the chair like a schoolgirl during breaks. Standing out in front, her movements become positively balletic. Soloists tend to have a repertoire of gestures and postures, but Julia, as well as directing with the bow, uses her whole body to carry the orchestra along. Standing at first feet together, or even with legs crossed, she will turn and swing a leg out towards the cellos, spin back to stand square with legs apart, then spin again to her right to make a point with the first

Julia Fischer directing in rehearsal: 'her movements became positively ballestic .'

7

violins. Sometimes – at least in rehearsal – she will whirl round a full 180 degrees to encourage the harpsichordist whose improvisatory chords chime through the texture of the strings. Her body and limbs flow like those of a martial arts expert; but her feet – and her Delphic smile – belong to the ballerina. Fischer's physical exuberance was explained when later I read in a magazine article that as a child she had been fascinated by figure-skating, and had to be dissuaded by her mother from taking it up full-time.

Staying sane on tour

In these days of marital equality and nuclear families, going on tour is a difficult separation. The story is told of a newly-married fiddle player who went to see Sylvia Holford, a former Academy manager, and lamented: 'There are twelve days in the year when my wife is most likely to conceive, and I'm away for eleven of them.' Once on the road, life boils down to basics. If silence and sleep are two of the most necessary items, food is surely the third. The quantity – and often quality – of American food can test the toughest metabolism. Everyone has to find their own solution. Breakfast is important; but hotel breakfasts are not always included in the room price, and can be expensive – which is why in the U.S. the players get a higher daily allowance than in Europe. One violinist quickly solved the problem by buying oatmeal and using the coffee percolator in her bedroom to make porridge every morning. Tea-drinkers have a hard time in America. You can get good breakfast tea in little muslin bags. But nobody seems to know that tea needs boiling water.

When so many hours are spent in airports, learning what to eat on the run is essential. Some go for pots of salad. Others head for the sushi bar – usually good and not expensive. Learning what to avoid is even more important. (My personal hate is Mexican food). It took my wife and I eight days to work out our feeding pattern. Because rehearsals are held before every concert, the players' evening meal is usually a cold buffet laid out on a trestle table backstage for them to pick at in the hour left for getting changed. The most vital commodity, it seems, is bananas.

What people do with their free time is a matter of temperament. Some (and not only the women) like to mosey round the clothes shops. Some look for vigorous exercise, hiring a bicycle or going for a long walk. Going for a walk is not something which Americans understand ('hiking' is what they do), and

A hurried snack between rehearsal and performance trumpeter Michael Laird.

the country is not designed for it. On their free day in Costa Mesa two of the viola players tried to beat the system. Skipping lunch, they hired a car planning to drive up into the mountains, take their walk, and eat a good meal. But they hadn't allowed for the California climate. Up there, they found the roads snowbound.

Some frequent the art galleries, some the bookshops. Some blow the whole of their *per diem* allowance on a three-course meal in the best restaurant in town.

But for others, this is all too fatiguing. They prefer to stay in their rooms, do a little practising – perhaps learning a piece they are due to play on the next tour – watching TV, wandering the Internet, sending emails, ordering meals from room service, and sleeping. The violinist Miranda Playfair told me she takes as many cat-naps as she can ('like a teenager,') but is prone to anxiety dreams in which she finds herself standing on stage about to play a concerto without a clue how the piece begins. (This, of course, is the musician's version of the Actor's Dream).

After their instruments, the players' most important items of equipment are a mobile phone, a laptop computer for watching movies and sending emails, or perhaps a Blackberry, and an iPod for listening to music. The invention of computer telephony has been a godsend to touring musicians. On one of the longer bus rides, a violinist who has two children and was expecting her third was able to use the wi-fi system to spend an hour talking to her children who, eight time zones away, had just come back from school. In the old days players scrambled to find a telephone kiosk - only to discover, perhaps, that the family was in the middle of some domestic crisis, and their absence was being blamed for it.

Some trawl the bookshops:
Robert Smissen, prinicpal
viola, waiting to go on.

In the old days, journeys would be shortened by games of bridge, poker or chess, extended jokes or quizzes. Hotel rooms were shared. (These days   players have rooms of their own) A typical packing list, according to one female cellist, consisted of: 'At least five good books, travelling kettle, Earl Grey teabags, pen-knife, corkscrew, "interesting" earrings, Elastoplast, Scrabble, hair gel, favourite jumper, teddy bear, hot water bottle, concert dresses, passport…oh, and cello.'[2]

For their wellbeing on tour, musicians depend greatly on the skill of their managers. On this tour the responsibility fell on four people: Tara Persaud, con-certs manager of the Academy; Nigel Barratt, the stage manager from London; Kay McCavic, company manager from the American agency Opus 3 Artists; and her colleague Gerald (Gerry) Breault, stage manager, immediately identifiable by his flat cap of Donegal tweed.

It is not usually the orchestral players who cause the trouble – as travellers they are too experienced to need nannying. Soloists can be difficult, however, if only because they tend to be even more detached from time and place. I heard that Murray Perahia, principal guest conductor of the Academy, can be found practising the piano at three in the morning and has to be reminded to get some sleep. Stage managers have to think of everything, from trundling double basses to replenishing the supply of bananas. Tact is needed when dealing with the unionized workers in American halls and theatres. Arriving at a hall, it is not safe to unload or move anything without permission. 'Union workers expect you to show complete respect for their territory,' Tara said. 'But if you do, they're

A cat-nap on the bus
to cope with jet-lag.

usually friendly.' Every concert is attended by the local fireman [firefighter] with the power to stop the show if he finds something wrong. A player rashly suggested to one of these officers that he must have got to learn a lot about classical music. 'I don't know nothin' about classical music,' he replied. 'All I know is that a piano burns in ten minutes and a violin in three.'

Spending most of their time on their mobile phones, Kay and Tara (who went everywhere at a run) were unflappable. That was remarkable, considering how easily things can go wrong. And, inevitably, they did go wrong.

The Academy's keyboard player John Constable, in charge of the harpsichord continuo for the Bach concerti, failed to catch the flight from London because his wife was in hospital with a worrying allergic reaction and he dared not leave her. Tara and Kay spent most of the band's first free day on the telephone looking for a substitute, and then, when they had found one, trying to locate a written-out part for her to play. (Continuo players are specialists who don't usually need a written part, but improvise from the orchestral score, supplying additional harmonies and so thickening the texture of the music like flour in a sauce). A substitute would have to be found for the next engagement, near Phoenix, Arizona; then there was San Francisco to come…. The two women were praying that Mrs. Constable would soon recover.

Medical emergencies are one kind of hazard. Others are lost luggage or – worse still – lost or damaged instruments.

Once when the band was travelling from London to Frankfurt, the cellos could not travel as passengers because there were too many of them. So they were packed in baskets, two to a basket, at Heathrow Airport. The basses travelled, as usual, in their big reinforced cases. When the consignment arrived in Frankfurt, one of the basses was found to be in a terrible state. The neck was snapped off and the body was drenched. It turned out that at the cargo shed the cello cases had been stacked together on a truck, with the bass wedged vertically between them. Coming out of the door of the shed the driver failed to check the clearance, and the bass was decapitated. Not content with that, handlers then stacked the instruments outside in the rain, so that the inside of the broken bass box was flooded. Lost instruments make good stories, of course, especially if they are Stradivarius violins worth millions of dollars, but are a waking nightmare for those to whom they are entrusted. Surprisingly often, there is a happy ending. [See *The Best Way to Lose a Cello*, Page 14]

John Constable, the Academy's keyboard player.
Photo: Mike Hoban

On European tours, the instruments usually travel separately by truck. The driver has a big responsibility, not only for the safety of the precious cargo, but for getting to the venues on time. For 30 years that job has been done for the Academy by Ian Bonner, known as 'Bonzo'. 'The truck runs on diesel and I run on goulasch,' he told me when we met over breakfast in Berlin. He was on his way to Budapest, and had a choice between what he called the 'bandit run' through the Czech Republic and Slovakia, or the longer, safer route through Germany and Austria. He would be driving at night in midwinter snow, and in his truck were, like the 'Twelve Days of Christmas': six violas, six cellos, three double basses, two bassoons, three French horns and two trumpets. Later I was told by Katherine Adams, who has looked after the orchestra on tour for almost as long as 'Bonzo', that he has a miraculous way with officialdom. 'He can deal with people of any country,' she said. 'He doesn't need to know languages. He talks about football, and has them eating out of his hand.'

Because of the dangers, some players refuse to take their best instruments on tour. On airplanes and buses, cellos usually sit next to their owners, like mute and faithful spouses. Airlines have no common policy on this, and check-in procedures can be complicated. One of the Academy's former bass players, Raymund Koster, got round the problem by taking with him a small Italian instrument which he told the airlines was a cello. No-one ever contradicted him.

Violins and violas will go in the overhead locker or luggage rack, though some airlines ban violas from the cabin.[3] Even there they are not entirely safe. On the second leg of this tour, from Phoenix to San Francisco, the principal viola Robert Smissen had a *mauvais quart d'heure* arriving at Oakland airport when an over-zealous passenger threw open the locker, and his viola fell out. Fortunately the instrument was in a metal case and its descent was interrupted by the head of another passenger. The first passenger excused himself to the furious second passenger, saying: 'Hey, how did I know it was in there!'. The injured party, still furious, claimed that he already suffered from a bad neck, and went straight to the flight attendant to lodge an 'incident report'. Perhaps he thought to make money out of it. Neither of them had a word of apology for the unfortunate owner of the viola, or stopped to see if the instrument had been damaged.

Despite having a similar name, our next stop, Mesa, was a quite different sort of place. Founded as a Mormon settlement in the Arizona desert, it has become a dormitory town for Phoenix, the state capital. Mesa was not only dry, it was hot – hot enough for shirtsleeves. Main Street was a dull little thoroughfare, apart from the concert hall in which the orchestra would be playing that night. You would never guess it was the hub of a large and expanding city of 450,000 people. I later discovered that, based on the amount of national news coverage it attracted the

[continued on page 16]

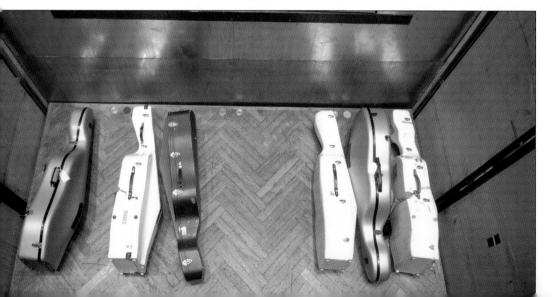

'Going up': cellos riding the lift backstage.

13

Denis Vigay.
Photo: Musica Viva Australia

The Best Way to Lose a Cello

Denis Vigay was on tour in America with the Academy Chamber Ensemble, usually known as The Octet. He had taken his own cello, a valuable Paulo Testore. This is how he tells the story:

'We were staying at a motel in Iowa, I remember, and after the concert were invited to a convivial reception at Des Moines University, where the wine flowed in generous abundance. Later in the evening we carried our instruments back to the motel, where I put the cello down and fell heavily asleep. The next day was a day off, so I got up late and looked round for my cello. There was no sign of it. Had I left it in the passage outside the room? It wasn't there either. I asked the others, but none of them had seen it. We rang the police and a policeman came: he was six foot two, with a stetson and a gun. He asked me: "What's a cello?". Then he noticed that the door of my room wouldn't lock.

'I could imagine my cello heading South and crossing the border to Mexico in the boot of a large American car. The police told me it would probably end up in a pawn shop. I had to phone ahead to organise a cello for the next concert. We were playing the Dvořák Quintet, I remember. Funnily enough, the cello they found for me was called 'Dvořák'. All my music was in my cello case, including a new octet by Kenneth Leighton (of which there was only one copy) due to be given a first performance at the Carnegie Hall a week later. Molly Marriner had to arrange to get another copy sent to me.

'Three days later, my cello was found in a cornfield near the hotel where the maize was ten feet high. A farmer on his combine was cutting down the autumn corn stalks when he spotted the cello lying on the ground in its fibreglass case. It was not even damp, and the strings were still in tune. And my music was still inside.'

Losing instruments on tour is not uncommon. An absent-minded soloist I know of lost two, leaving both his violin and viola in a London taxi – from which they were recovered. But losing a player is rather more unusual. Many years ago, in the 1970s, the Academy was travelling by train from Germany to Austria. One of its violinists was Josef Fröhlich, a refugee from Eastern Europe, who had been issued with an international passport.

In the middle of the night Austrian border police came onto the train at Passau to inspect passports. They didn't like the look of Fröhlich's, and took him off. The Marriners were woken by a frantic hammering on their compartment door. It was the viola player Anthony Jenkins, who told them what had happened, and relayed Frölich's message: Nothing could be done . . . go on to Vienna. On arrival in Vienna, Neville rang the British Ambassador and told him to let it be known that the Academy would not play a note until their missing violinist was returned to them.

Meanwhile, back in Passau, the head of the border police told Frölich his passport was fine, gave him money and a ticket and put him on the next train to Vienna, where Molly Marriner met him just in time for him to take his place for the concert.

[continued from page 13]

previous year, Mesa had been rated by *Forbes*, the business magazine, as the most 'boring' of the bigger U.S cities. It was odd that the Academy, which a few weeks before I had watched perform in Vienna's Musikverein – 'the world capital of music' – was tonight appearing in this dull desert dormitory. But Mesa was more musical than I realised. The barmaid who conjured up a beer and out-of-hours sandwich for me in the bistro on Main Street turned out to be an amateur cellist. She was going to the concert, she told me. And a few yards down the street I found the largest music shop I have seen anywhere – two floors of instruments, accessories and sheet music – with a warehouse next door and a piano store across the road, behind which I found a row of practice cubicles and a waiting room full of young mothers. The shop assistant – another cellist – explained that Mesa had a big schools music programme, and that we were standing in the largest music store in the state of Arizona. She knew all about Neville Marriner and the Academy of St Martin in the Fields, but was astonished to learn that the orchestra was in town. The people at the concert hall were not very good at publicity, she said apologetically, and the enthusiasm of Mesa's schoolteachers and parents didn't always extend to taking the children to concerts.

Yet that night, when I joined the crowd waiting for the auditorium doors to open, there were lots of schoolchildren. The hall – a 1,600-seater – was still only half full, however, and I learned that 400 of the tickets had been handed out free. It didn't seem to matter. The enthusiasm was palpable. Behind me I heard a man reading from the programme to his wife: 'Hey, it says here the orchestra wasn't founded in the fields, but some place in London.' Not for the first time – and surely not for the last – was the orchestra's name found puzzling.

Last minute adjustments: Michael Laird adjusts John Heley's bow-tie.

After the band had taken the stage, Julia appeared in floaty black trousers to loud applause, paused to smile at the audience, sat down and plunged straight into the Britten. During the interval, I noticed, people were drinking mineral water. Very few bought the white wine on offer. I picked a concertgoer at random, and asked him what he thought. 'Amazing,' was the reply. 'The way they start, and move, and stop all together. Amazing.' The compliment appreciated considerably in value when I learned that my interlocutor was the principal second violinist of the Symphony of the Southwest, the orchestra based at this hall. Back at the hotel, having a drink with some of the players, I said how lively I thought the performance had been. 'Was it? Glad you thought so,' said one. 'I was half asleep most of the time.' He was joking, of course, but the jet lag was certainly still at work.

The following morning, bright and warm again, we were driven back across the desert, past an Indian Reservation, to Phoenix airport for the flight to Oakland and San Francisco. There would be a free evening, and nothing the following day until 4 p.m. when the band would be taken across the Bay to rehearse and play at the big Zellerbach concert hall at the University of California, Berkeley.

It was Valentine's Day, and on the bus ride over there was debate about the deeper significance of a text message which one of the girls had found on her mobile. Valentine's Day may also have explained the big turn-out that greeted us. Before the concert I was introduced to the impresario Robert Cole, who had fond memories of Neville Marriner and wanted to be remembered to him. They had first met in Los Angeles in the 1970s. Cole is a conductor who in 1986 took over the running of Cal Performances for the university at Berkeley, cultivating so many international stars – he plays the occasional round of golf with Mikhail Baryshnikov – that Berkeley is now considered one of the top music, dance and jazz venues outside New York.

I asked him how he rated the Academy. 'Compared with others? Gosh, I don't think there is another chamber orchestra which has established the kind of name recognition that it has,' he said. 'Neville always had the choice of the best players in London. And the freelance musicians in London are the best, pretty much, in the world.'

The reviewer for the *San Francisco Chronicle* seemed inclined to agree. The Academy could sometimes sound 'pleasantly bland', he wrote next day, but 'Fischer deployed all of the orchestra's greatest virtues – its clarity and rhythmic precision, the vivacious brightness of its instrumental colours . . . There was a new sense of urgency.' Another reviewer denounced the 'bland' barb, likening the players' approach to the Britten to a tiger attacking a chunk of raw meat. Their performance was 'tight, passionate and scalding hot,' she wrote, and astonishing for an orchestra without a conductor.

Over drinks back at the hotel, the players moodily contemplated the next leg of the tour. We were to leave at 8 a.m., fly to Seattle, and take a bus from Seattle airport over the border into Canada, a four-hour road journey, arriving in Vancouver barely in time for a rehearsal scheduled for half past five. The concert was at eight. 'I wouldn't bother with Vancouver if I were you,' Stephen Orton said. When I demurred he said: 'Let's put it to the vote,' and turned to the other players at the table. Secretly, my wife and I had already considered skipping Vancouver to spend the extra time in Seattle, where the band was due to return the following day. We reasoned that we would see nothing but the inside of a concert hall, and a hotel. The only reason for going was solidarity, to share the players' ordeal.

The vote was unanimous that we skip Vancouver. And thankful we were to take the advice when two days later we heard what happened. Customs clearance had taken an hour and a half – it seems the paperwork for the double basses was to blame – and the band did not get to Vancouver until 6 p.m. They had 20 minutes in which to wash and rest, then took a quick rehearsal and a bite of pizza backstage before dressing up and going out to play.

The apparent reason for the strange manoeuvre was that the airline on which the orchestra had been block-booked would not allow more than two cellos and one double bass on a flight into Canada. Since there were three cellos and two double basses in the band, that would have meant dividing the party and booking two flights to Vancouver. So the bus journey was substituted.

On their return the players were not amused. 'It was a risky decision the management made,' said one. 'We could easily have missed the concert altogether. As it was, we arrrived tired out.' Meanwhile, my wife and I had been enjoying ourselves in Seattle, home of the Boeing aircraft company, of Bill Gates the mogul of Microsoft, and of the ubiquitous Starbucks coffee shop chain. We ate on the waterfront, visited the fish market, browsed the Elliott Bay Bookstore on Pioneer Square, and took a ferry ride over to Bainbridge Island where we had lunch and walked among trees on real grass for the first time in a week. (How deeply we country-dwellers feel the lack of greenery on our travels!) Although a Monday, this was a national holiday – President's Day – and therefore well-timed for the Academy's appearance that night at the splendid Benaroya Hall on Second Avenue, purpose-built for concerts.

After the performance a fleet of taxis was marshalled to take us to a party at the house of Gerard ('Gerry') Schwarz, longtime music director of the Seattle Symphony (Boeing, Bill and Mrs Gates and Microsoft all appear among its patrons), and also a friend of the Academy. Schwarz succeeded Neville Marriner as music director of the Los Angeles Chamber Orchestra.

The Schwarzes live on the heights of Seattle with a splendid view of the Sound and a splendid collection of oil paintings and exotic ornaments. As we sat with plates of hot food on our laps, I heard from Jody, Mrs. Schwarz, how her husband had led the Seattle musicians out of the American trade union so that they could take on more, and more various, kinds of work. Although engaged full time with the Seattle Symphony, they enjoyed in this respect some of the freedom and variety of the Academy's freelances, she said. It was hard for symphonic players in America to emulate the enthusiasm and musicianship which distinguished the Academy, because under contract they do four concerts a week, thirty-two weeks a year, and are – as she put it – 'just cranking out the music.'

The drink flowed, and Gerry, presented with a thank-you bottle of champagne, made a little speech. 'You are not just great players, not just virtuosi, but great musicians,' he said. 'With other orchestras you often wonder what is going on inside the players' heads – if anything at all. With you, it's the phrasing which marks you out, telling the story – which is what music is about.'

Not surprisingly, this went down very well. I had the feeling that tonight, in the fifth concert of the tour, the band had really hit its stride. The reviewer on a music website wrote that he found many moments in the music 'realized more vividly than I had ever heard them played before,' and praised Julia's direction of what he called 'a string orchestra of transcendent calibre.'

We descended through Denver City's notoriously bumpy airspace an hour or so after the new president of the United States, Barack Obama, who had flown in to explain his national economic rescue plan to an audience of Colorado businessmen. The soup kitchen queue we observed in the gathering dusk on our drive into the city centre was a foretaste of what the country would soon be suffering in the recession triggered by the reckless handling of debt by some of the world's biggest banks. Obama, we later discovered, had just left for Mesa, Arizona, where we had been four days before. I wondered if our two caravans would eventually collide…

Although strung out for miles beneath the eastern escarpment of the Rocky Mountains, Denver has a pleasant city centre built over the old cowboy town, bisected by a tree-lined pedestrian mall whose free municipal bus runs from the railroad station to the state Capitol. After checking in, we rushed out to find dinner, accompanied by Steve Orton and two of the glamour girls from the first violins. A nearby seafood restaurant displayed a fish tank with two lobsters scrabbling halfheartedly at the glass: it was enough to persuade the musicians to stay. But we pressed on, ending up in a noisy, cheap but cheerful steak-and-shrimp diner where a very gay waiter entertained us with local gossip and huge Margaritas. Recession or not, life felt good.

Denver was to be our base for three nights and for two concerts in outlying towns: Beaver Creek, a small but plush ski resort in the Rockies, over the Continental Divide near Vail; and, much closer, the University of Colorado campus at Boulder.

Next morning I saw that the tour schedule for Beaver Creek carried a warning: 'Please note that this venue is situated at an altitude of 2500 metres above sea level.' Since Denver is known as Mile-High City, it was not surprising that a resort at the top of the Rockies should be that much higher. The significance of the warning, however, was only to become apparent later.

Few journeys can be more pleasant than a gentle bus ride through mountain scenery on a good road devoid of hairpin bends. It began to snow as we climbed, passing the ruins of quaintly-named mining towns opened 150 years ago by gold-hungry speculators from the east. By degrees, the sky darkened, the snow thickened, and we began to wonder whether we should get back to Denver that night.

In the dusk, the resort of Beaver Creek looked smart but soul-less: rows of grey stone apartment buildings and villas of uniform design. From a side door of the arts centre building we descended many flights to the green room, three levels down beneath the concert hall. Buried in the mountainside, the auditorium was small, opulent and cozy. At the start of a short rehearsal, Harvey de Souza went again to the back of the auditorium to listen, reporting that the double basses were resonating tremendously. 'It sounds like six basses from up there,' he said. This may have been due partly to the big wooden screen immediately behind them which acted as a soundboard.

While the players changed, we went up for air. The back stairwell led to a steel-plated door in a hatch. Opening it, we stepped out to find ourselves in a picture from a Christmas storybook. We were at the edge of a snow-covered ice-rink around which a few small children in furry suits and hoods were circling. The rink was illuminated by the buildings which crowded in on all sides – brand new, but quaintly designed with overhanging eaves and high gables to suggest some remote village in the Austrian Alps. Instead of the jovial piemaker and the bespectacled cobbler, however, we found the art dealer and the luxury furrier. The art gallery, owned by an an English dealer, was stocked mainly with landscapes in oils selling for around $30,000 apiece. Next door was one of Beaver Creek's several fur shops: the plump and pretty saleswoman had no customers, and seized a beaver coat to throw around my wife. The price tag said $3,000, reduced from $8,000.

Returning to the subterranean hall we found the players milling about backstage, warming up on their instruments. But there was anxiety in the air. This was explained when Steve Orton came up waving a rubbery snake-like object with beads at each end.

'Do you know what this is?' he asked.

'Haven't a clue,' we said.

'It's a humidifier.'

We might have been below ground, but we were so far above sea-level that the air was crackling dry. The players feared for their instruments. In such conditions, a fiddle can literally fall apart. The point of the snake was to douse it in water and put it inside the violin or cello in order to keep the wood moist. The front and back panels of a fiddle are only lightly glued to the sides, so that under climatic duress they will separate instead of the wood splitting. Once the seams come apart, the instrument is useless, and must be taken to an expert for repair.

This ungluing can occur even at sea-level, especially in overheated American hotel rooms and apartments during winter. It happened to Arnold Steinhardt, leader of the Guarneri String Quartet, when he was a student in Philadelphia, as he recounts in his memoir:

'On one bitterly cold morning, an oddly thin and hollow sound dribbled out of my Dollenz [a 19th-century violin from Trieste], as if it was being played in the next room. I discovered that a section of the violin's ribs directly to the side of the chin rest had separated slightly from the back, to which it was glued . . . The unexpected opening in my Dollenz, barely wide enough to slip a razor blade inside, played havoc with the sound.'[4]

Strange sounds from the stage cannot be explained to an audience: and it is easy to see how damaging such sounds would be to an orchestra with an international reputation. And in that small concert hall, the impact of the band - quite apart from the resounding basses – was going to be exceptional. And so it proved. During the interval I spoke to a member of the audience who thought the opening bars of the Britten were out of tune. Had he picked up on the effects of altitude? His wife, who was a violinist, did not agree with her husband. Perhaps it was unfamiliar dissonances he was hearing.

As the band packed up to leave, the snow looked ever more threatening. Julia decided not to take the car back down to Denver but seek the greater safety of the bus. The concert had been scheduled early, so it was still only about 9 p.m. when we set off. Now we heard that earlier in the evening a man in the audience had been spotted with a video camera. Challenged by a member of staff he claimed that whatever he had filmed was now erased. But when the camera was inspected, it was found to have a recording of the concert still on it. Covert filming and taping might be regarded as a tribute, a harmless display of enthusiasm. But of course musicians, especially well-known soloists, don't think so. Like other peformers, they depend on royalties from legal recordings and broadcasts; we were told that Anne-Sophie Mutter, the German violinist protégé of von Karajan, became obsessively watchful for breaches of copyright. Before her concerts, halls had to be searched for hidden microphones and audiences were frisked for hidden equipment.

After a few miles, as the road began to climb up again to the Continental Divide, the driver stopped in a layby to put on his snow chains. He clearly thought the snow was not bad enough to justify them but, as he explained, if the traffic cops catch you without them on this stretch, you pay a large fine. A number of the players climbed out of the bus to inhale the swirling snowflakes. I found the driver crouching by a wheel, and offered to lend a hand. But there was only one wheel to be fitted, and we were soon on our way. I began to realise the enormous responsibility taken by drivers. This man was answerable not just for the lives of the 30 people on board, including the best string players in Britain and a young soloist of international stature. He was also carrying a lot of precious instruments, with a collective value of perhaps more than £2.25 million. One of the cellos, I know, was alone worth £400,000. And as for Julia's Guadagnini violin of 1742, it might be twice that. Watching the driver wrestling with his chains, I imagined the consequences if the bus fell off the mountain and began to understand why tour managers say the bus driver is the most important person in the party.

Another splendid concert hall greeted us on the campus at Boulder. Outside, it looked like a chunk of Hampton Court Palace. Inside, the 2,050-seater Macky Auditorium was more like a Gaumont cinema, with Arab-style motifs breaking up its cream-coloured surfaces. Julia arrived at the rehearsal swinging her hips skittishly. The serious young German that critics write about is ready enough to laugh and play games when she is with people she knows. Tonight she was clearly in good form. At one point in the Britten she stopped to ask the cellos what they were doing with a particular phrase: 'Should this be crescendo, or decrescendo – piano to pianissimo – followed by a crescendo? I don't mind which it is, as long as it is *something.*' When the bar was played again, the four violins behind Julia stood up as one as if to drive the point home.

The audience that night was much bigger and livelier than at Beaver Creek, not surprisingly since the concert had been put on by the university's music school. Among the crowd were most of the school's double bass students, led by their teacher. Earlier in the afternoon, in response to a last-minute invitation

[continued on page 26]

The expert:
Simon Morris, a
player turned dealer.

Photo: J & A Beare

Partners for life?

Musicians sometimes talk about their instruments as if they were lovers. Searching for a violin or cello is like looking for a mate. Selling one is like getting a divorce, when you have grown apart, or fallen out of love. Instruments are usually faithful, even when their owners are not. But they can also play up, says Helen Paterson, owner of an early 18th Century Camillus Camilli from Mantua, 'When that happens you wonder: Is it the violin? Or is it me? Is it the wood, or the strings, or the bow? Or the temperature? Or the weather?'. Martin Loveday, who has a valuable Alexander Gagliano cello of 1724, concurred: 'Some days you wonder whether there isn't a crack in the wood. And then two hours later the cello starts to make a wonderful sound, and you don't know what caused the problem.' Arnold Steinhardt writes in his memoir that even if a violin is perfectly set up, it sounds different every day of the year because of changes in pressure, temperature or humidity. 'The violin is a surprisingly delicate instrument.'

One who knows just how delicate is Simon Morris, a former Academy cellist and director of London violin dealers John & Arthur Beare. He recalls on US tours struggling to keep his hotel room humid: he would stand his cello in the bathroom with the bath full of water. 'Real changes do happen,' he told me, when I went to consult him in his London office. 'The neck might move, changing the position of the strings relative to the fingerboard. Or the glue can dry out where the front meets the sides, and you get a buzz.'

As for the tricks an instrument plays on its owner, he told me, that was mostly subjective. 'Because I work with so many different instruments, I don't have that sensitivity – or neurosis, if you like.' Musicians and their instruments are like couples who live together, he said: they get oversensitive to each other. Players are aware of the smallest change in the instrument, changes which would be undetectable to someone standing six feet away. 'On top of that, it's easy to transfer your own inadequacies to the instrument. We are like tennis players who come on court with ten racquets. They pick one up, reject it, then take another one which is exactly the same. You become sensitized to the tools that you use. It's inevitable when you play so much.'

Like motor cars in the old days, stringed instruments have to be 'run in'. After an overhaul – new fittings or strings – they have to be played in to get them resonating properly. That job requires a good technique, because playing scratchily or out of tune will put the instrument out too. (Don't be offended, therefore, if a professional refuses to let you have a go on their Strad). The first time I met Harvey de Souza he was playing in a Guarneri violin for Beare's. The soundbox 'needs to remember how to sound', I was told.

Many string players have two instruments: one for touring, one for home; or because they switch between 'period' and modern orchestras, like Miranda Playfair, another of the Academy's first violins. Old instruments can be quirky, she says, and you have to be on form to play them. 'Most soloists keep a modern violin in the cupboard.'

Everyone agrees that violins from the so-called Golden Age in Italy (17th and early 18th centuries) have never been surpassed. But nobody knows why. What's the secret of Stradivarius? 'You might as well ask: what's the secret of Michelangelo,' Simon Morris said. 'Did he have a special chisel? No. Antonio Stradivari was brought up in an age when there was no such thing as a bad violin.' Players buy old instruments for their sound. And also, of course, for their value. It's their pension.

During one of the Academy's U.S. tours three of the violinists went out and bought a new fiddle each. Within a few years all three tried to sell them. With new instruments the initial impression is very good, Morris explained. They make a good sound, loud and soft, and all that you need for modern-day concert halls. But the 'colour' of the sound can be one-dimensional, and after six months or a year frustration sets in because the player cannot get the palette of colours that an old instrument provides.

Theories abound as to why old Italian violins are best. Some say it's the result of the logs from which they were made absorbing seawater as they were transported to dock; others the tightness of the grain in the spruce grown during a mini Ice Age of the 18th century; others point to volcanic ash in the varnish. None is a sufficient explanation. 'If it had just been the quality of the materials we would have replicated that by now. No-one wants to acknowledge the simple truth, that the violin makers of that time in Italy were just extremely good at what they did. The secret of Stradivarius is the man himself.'

[continued from page 23] by e-mail, the two touring bassists, Lynda Houghton and Catherine Elliott, had gone up to the school to impart to the students some of the secrets of playing without a conductor (secrets which will be revealed in the next chapter). Both women take a keen interest in music education. Lynda, as well as being an Academy principal and one of three player-members of the Board, is also the first woman to have played double bass for the London Symphony Orchestra.

At Denver airport the following morning I had a chance to talk to Julia Fischer. Having watched her at work now for 12 days, I was curious to hear how the orchestra looked from her point of view.

Julia first played with the Academy in 2001 when she was a teenager, and recorded Vivaldi's *Four Seasons* with them on DVD. Since then she has led a number of tours and appeared with the bigger Academy orchestra under Neville Marriner. It was with him conducting the Junge Deutsche Philharmonie at the Alte Oper in Frankfurt that she planned a surprise debut as a concert pianist in January 2008. (Julia has played the piano alongside the violin from an early age). The plan was for her to perform the Saint-Saens Violin Concerto No. 3 in B minor, then reappear as what had been billed as a 'mystery soloist' in Grieg's Piano Concerto in A minor. When Neville had to withdraw before the concert, to look after Molly who had cracked her knee, Julia was distraught. The double solo went ahead as planned, however, under Matthias Pintscher.

Perfect unison: Neville Marriner rehearsing with Julia Fischer.

An incidental connection was that before she got her Guadagnini – it lay on the seat beside her as we talked – Julia had for five years been playing the Stradivarius which once belonged to Iona Brown, director of the Academy after Neville went off to pursue a conducting career.

I asked Julia if she divided responsibility for the interpretation of the music with the orchestra. 'Yes I do, in the sense that I value everyone's opinion and want to know what they think,' she said. 'Even if they disagree with me, I want them to feel free to speak.' For the Bach concertos her interpretation as the soloist would naturally prevail. But in the Britten and Walton, at least at the start of the two tours, she deferred to them because they knew the pieces much better than she did. 'During this tour my own interpretation has come through more. The orchestra realise that I have a view.' I observed that at every rehearsal so far she seemed to have a list of points to make. Did she go through the scores every day in her hotel room? Sometimes, she said, but not necessarily with the score. She has every note of them in her head.

The Academy is the only orchestra she has directed. What she likes about it is its democratic spirit: 'This degree of democracy is only possible where everyone respects everyone else, and of course with the level of players you have there. In many orchestras the principals are fantastic but as you go towards the back desks it gets more mediocre. Here you could turn everyone around.'

I asked if at this stage of a tour things began to slip. 'It depends on the pieces,' she replied. 'You always need to practise, just as if you are a soloist. There is no perfect concert. That means something goes wrong in every concert. That means you have to look at it again every night.'

I wondered if the individualism of the Academy players could cause slippages.

'I wouldn't think so. Because with this individuality also comes the ability to listen to others.'

'They say the fact that you are so young is irrelevant. Is that true,?'

'Yes, that's true.'

'What is it that counts, then?'

'Knowledge, experience, personality, dedication…'

'Are there any tricks you use to maintain harmony in the band?'

'Not with this one. They are not children.'

Julia has another tour with the Academy planned for March, 2011 and said she saw no reason not to continue playing and recording with them, in spite of her fast-developing solo career and her teaching job at another Academy – that for Music and the Performing Arts in Frankfurt, where she is Germany's youngest professor. 'I always have time for anything I want to do,' she said firmly. 'And this is something which is on my priority list.'

On we flew, to Kansas City for a three-night stay and two concerts, one of them out on the prairie. The players were beginning to feel the strain. One was just recovering from a stomach bug, others had sore fingers, stiff necks and shoulders. They had done a lot of playing in two back-to-back tours, with only a short break in the middle. Almost as soon as we arrived, Steve Orton was out on reconnaissance for a restaurant, to make the most of a concert-free evening. The next rehearsal was 24 hours away.

The centre of Kansas City, like most American cities, is quite small. It consists of a few square miles on a slope running down to the freeway to the east and the Missouri River to the north. Within a few minutes, led by Steve and John Constable the harpsichordist, we were down in the so-called Power and Light district, described by the city authorities as the Mid-West's 'premier entertainment epicenter.' But because this is God-fearing Missouri, the behaviour code is strict: among the prohibitions are: 'loitering, panhandling, solicitation; concealed weapons, bicycles and skateboards.'

But the promise outweighed the prohibitions. Across the street from the neon-lit 'epicenter' we came to our destination, the Bristol Seafood Grill, the best restaurant we had seen on the tour so far, by a wide margin.

Next morning, I walked out into the corridor and heard Martin Burgess, principal second violin, practising in the room opposite. The sound was barely audible – for the good reason that the fiddle was being played with a mute. Made of rubber or metal, these practice mutes look like primitive combs, and sit on the strings at the bridge. You can buy a heavyweight chrome-plated version designed specially for hotel rooms and apartment blocks. Players on tour always carry these devices.

Like a few members of the band, we decided to make an excursion today. The sun was out, but it was very cold. We shivered in the lee of a downtown office block – these steel-and-glass canyons create a vicious turbulence of their own – for an express bus that would take us a few miles south to the Nelson-Atkins Museum. We had been told by a painter friend that it contained the best collection of Chinese art in America. It also has a good collection of Henry Moore pieces, and some of his big sculptures in the grounds .

The ride proved as instructive as the museum itself. From the city centre the bus made its way down Main Street through acres of industrial dereliction: abandoned factories, rusted girders piled in deserted lots, broken windows and crumbling tenements. Here, as in many American cities, the old is left behind to rot, the new is built on the ever-expanding periphery. It is the same for the people: the poor and the immigrant remain, the upwardly mobile move out to the new condominiums and the covered shopping malls two, three or more miles away. Our fellow passengers were all black, and in various states of disrepair. The driver – also black –was a hearty woman who kept us entertained with her running commentary. We passed the magnificent railroad station, which, with the Missouri River was the reason for Kansas City's success as a trading post. On a flat piece of wasteland a shambling figure of a man waited for the bus, but at the wrong stop. At an intersection he caught up, and the driver let him board. It was an act of mercy; for the poor fellow was obviously demented.

We returned in a taxi. The band was performing that night in the Folly Theatre, a small and steeply-raked auditorium which the players said they preferred acoustically to the nearby concert hall. Their sound was warm, even intimate, and the detail more graphic. It may have been just my impression; but knowing the tour was coming to an end, the players seemed closer to each other than ever.

Sunday was our last day with the band. They were playing an afternoon concert at Columbia, Missouri, a two-and-a half-hour bus ride away. Not because we were tired of the programme – we were hearing new things each time – but because we were tired of travelling, we decided to play truant once more and take another day off.

At a side door of the Roman Catholic Cathedral of the Immaculate Conception, two blocks from our hotel, there was a queue of poor blacks waiting for food. On the roof of the cathedral glittered a cupola covered in gold leaf. Inside, a High School choir accompanied by violin, flute, piano, drums and occasionally tubular bells, sang raggedly from the gallery under a sky-blue vault. The organist could scarcely refrain from pulling out his prize stop: a battery of silver trumpets located above the altar. An old lady – the only black person visible in the congregation – shuffled forward to light a candle. Inside the front cover of the Mass book was a prayer to the Mother of God, asking her to help the cathedral overcome its overdraft problem.

Here, in Kansas City as in Orange County or in Denver, the signs of poverty clashed with the symbols of wealth. So they do in Britain, of course, and elsewhere in Europe. But there is something insouciant about the Americans' tolerance of blatant inequality – the kind of insouciance you see in India, and some other developing countries – which is quite foreign to us Europeans. Rich Americans don't seem troubled by bread queues – and they certainly don't like paying taxes. But they do give massively to support the arts. It is almost compulsory: once you have made a pile, you support the local 'symphony'. If you don't, you risk social ostracism. And so everywhere we travelled we saw magnificent theatres, concert halls and picture galleries fit to adorn any capital city in Europe.

We celebrated our last night in the hotel bar. Although the orchestra had one more engagement – in Bethesda, Maryland – Tara decided to make this the end-of-tour party. Over bottles of wine and plates of snacks, there were speeches. The writer thanked the musicians for accepting him and his wife into their family, and for letting them hear their music. Bob Smissen replied with his customary humour, and went on to praise Julia. As it happened, this was the night of the Oscar ceremonies in Los Angeles, and the plasma TV screen in the corner of the room was broadcasting, in exaggerated miniature, parallel rites of mutual congratulation. Julia seized the opportunity to make her own mock-Oscar speech pretending to fight back the tears.

It was a happy night, which made the next morning's parting more sorrowful.

We said goodbye on the airport bus – they were flying to Washington DC, we were going to New York. Musicians may seem exotic to the rest of us – their world is so different from ours – but they make wonderful travelling companions.

A week later, back in England, we got an email from Steve Orton. The final concert had been held in a beautiful hall, he wrote, with 'an acoustic to put our English halls to shame.' The band had enjoyed two nights of unexpected luxury, in the Ritz-Carlton Hotel in Georgetown: a big log fire in the lobby and ten pillows on every bed. Stephen had gone with the four band members who make up the Emperor Quartet – Martin Burgess, Clare Hayes, Fiona Bonds and William Schofield – to a jazz club round the corner where a young but 'rather tame' group played Thelonius Monk.

Reviewers of the Academy's American tour seemed surprised – even stunned – by the playing of the orchestra under Julia Fischer's direction. One or two found the Bach too austere for their taste; others thought it sublime. Almost all were carried away by the energy and attack of the strings in the Britten and Walton pieces. 'Scarily good playing,' said the reviewer for the *San Francisco Classical Voice*. 'This orchestra breathes and bows as one.' 'Sculpted readings that also breathed,' said the *Orange County Register*, 'and all accomplished with the merest nods and looks between these musicians.' *The Washington Post* used the word 'stunning', and wondered how the players managed, at the end of their tour, still to appear 'excited by their own musicmaking and by Fischer's musical ideas.'

How these qualities of togtherness, accuracy, tunefulness, urgency, variety and consistency are achieved – and all without a conductor – is what the next chapter will attempt to explain.

Chapter Two

INSIDE THE ENGINE

Every successful institution has its guiding principles and traditions. An orchestra is no exception. Indeed, as we shall see, orchestra are now being seen in some business quarters as a model of how successful institutions work.

There are three basic requirements for excellence in orchestral playing: first-class technique, perfect teamwork, and very good ears. But the fourth thing, the intangible thing, which distinguishes one orchestra from another, is the ethos or *esprit de corps* which keeps the show on the road.

And indeed, the Academy as a musical machine has often been likened to a Rolls-Royce: smooth, polished (the sound is sometimes called 'shiny'), elegant and utterly reliable.[1] But when it performs as a chamber orchestra without a conductor, you must think of it as a Rolls-Royce that dispenses with the chauffeur and drives itself.

The Academy sound will be familiar to all those who have collected its recordings since the 1960s – and to the millions who still hear those recordings on classical radio channels in Britain, the U.S. and Germany. Familiarity is both a challenge and a handicap. It is a challenge because audiences will expect nothing less than what they have heard on records. And it is a handicap if critics go to its concerts with a preconception of what they are going to hear. Matthew Ward, one of the youngest Academy players, recalls a disappointing review from a critic during a lively US tour with Joshua Bell as soloist-director: 'The critic obviously knew the Academy's sound from recordings of Mozart in the 70s and 80s. He just sort of pulled out an old review, talking about the 'Rolls-Royce of sound' and it not being very dynamic. But we there with this small, very dynamic group, and they were some of the most exciting concerts I've played in.'

The Academy sound is light, bright, clean, and precise, not just in the first and second violins, but all the way down. This sound has descended from the Academy's earliest days: a style of playing adopted for its revival of the Italian and German Baroque, but refined by the classical repertoire of Haydn and Mozart.

As they demonstrated with the Britten and Walton pieces on their American tour, the players' vigour is undiminished. Back in London I heard them give another dazzling display, at a thinly-attended Cadogan Hall concert: a sweet and touching rendition of Mozart's *Divertimento in D major* was followed by a psychedelic – ('raunchy' said one player) – performance of Piazolla's tango-inspired *Cuatras Estaciones Portenas* ('Four Seasons of Buenos Aires') with Julian Rachlin, arranged by Leonid Desyatnikov for violin and string orchestra. It received a standing ovation.

Before the concert I asked Julian Rachlin for his views on the Academy. 'No matter which format they are in , there is always the same excitement and a kind of passion and curiosity which the players project when you work with them,' he said. 'You never see them kind of leaning back, which you do in many

Julian Rachlin, soloist: 'I feel I am part of them'.
Photo: Pavel Antonov

other orchestras. This is the most strking thing about this orchestra, whether you are playing with them or directing them: everyone has to be treated as an individual because they are very fine musicians with their own ideas and personalities. It really starts to feel like a family. Often as a soloist you feel a bit detached. Not in this case. I feel I am part of them.'

Kenneth Sillito, who directs the chamber orchestra and leads the symphony orchestra (both from the front desk), says the Academy always has much the same sound whoever is directing or conducting

Kenneth Sillito and
Harvey de Souza.
Photo: Christian Tyler

it. And personnel changes over the years make no difference – something American audiences always comment on. The veteran violinist Malcolm Latchem, whose career with the Academy spanned 45 years, likes to compare it with the table in Salisbury Cathedral which is supposed to be over a thousand years old. Every bit of wood has been replaced at some time, but it remains the same table. To say there has been little change in the Academy sound is no disparagement, said Ken Sillito. 'It's to our credit. Any decent musical outfit has to have its own identity; and in music the identity is the sound, what people hear. Ours has been described as a 'white' sound. That does not mean it is colourless, but that it is not self-indulgent or idiosyncratic.'

The Academy style, epecially in the Baroque repertoire, is to articulate with the bow in a very precise manner, to remove 'that blurring at the edges that is typical of the symphony orchestra, where the audience gets more of a cushion of sound, more atmosphere, than individual notes.'

The man responsible for pioneering the new style agrees that although his successors, Iona Brown and Ken Sillito, have had their own ideas, the sound of the Academy is much as it always was. Marriner defines the the unifying characteristic as 'transparency', a word popular with the orchestra, but easier to demonstrate on the fiddle than to put into words. These are Neville's words for it:

'When I was a student, early music like Bach was heavy, ponderous, thick. In England there was a tradition of playing Bach as serious, Handel as boisterous. So the Bach was too slow and the Handel too noisy. Thanks to my experience with Bob [Thurston] Dart, the first of the English musicologists, this transparency became the key element of what we were looking for.

It requires a certain lightness and virility of the violin stroke, enormous energy but not heavy, thick or dense. And once you get it in the upper strings, you demand it from the lower. Then you add the wind, making sure they don't play everything *sostenuto*. There has to be a certain bite to the sound, but then you have got to release it a little bit so that you can hear other things going on which I would consider more important things. When a wind player sees a long note, he plays it long but there is filigree going on elsewhere in the orchestra. We began to insist that they sustain the note but *fortepiano* – not loud all the time, but with a *subito* [sudden] attack and then release so you can hear what's going on inside the harmony.'[2]

What Neville is describing here in his matter-of-fact way is nothing less than a stylistic revolution. Just how much of a revolution was brought home to his wife Molly on an occasion she will never forget. She was at a dinner party at the flat of Lynn Harrell, the celebrated American cellist who was then head of the Royal Academy of Music, arranged for him by his wife Linda for his birthday. Alfred Brendel was there with his wife Renée, and in Neville's absence – he was away somewhere – they began to discuss how he had 'changed string-playing in England.'

Defined by Neville's approach to the Baroque, this style was carried from the chamber orchestra to the symphony orchestra, from the strings to the wind players, and later to the Academy chorus whose voices were chosen for their light timbre and lack of operatic colour so that they, too, would match the strings.

Neville had in his ear the sound of a particular singer: the English counter-tenor Alfred Deller, whose voice seemed to him completely right for early music. 'The sort of noise he made I wanted to do on the violin,' he told me.

But the great influence was Robert Thurston Dart, whom Neville met quite by accident during the Second World War. The two men found themselves in adjacent beds in a nursing home in Kent where both were recuperating from wounds. Thurston Dart was three years older, a Cambridge mathematician planning to move into music, and it was his enthusiasm for the Baroque that first infected Neville: 'Bob Dart showed us how to adapt performing conventions of

'Bob' Thurston Dart at the
clavichord while Thomas
Goff, its maker, looks on.

Photo: Argo

the period without interfering with the way we played our instruments for the
rest of the time. He persuaded us to play with Corelli bows – the ones that look
like they should have arrows to go with them – gut strings and lower-pitched
instruments. We got the feel of what it was like to play the repertoire on old instruments, however, and then adjusted articulation and vibrato on our modern
instruments.'[3] One of the tricks was to use the point of the bow, never the heel,
to get an 'attack-less' sound.

The point was that most of the Academy's regulars then, unlike now, made
their living playing for symphony orchestras, and it was too much to ask them
to swap from one instrument to another. Later, with the proliferation of 'period
instrument' orchestras, a few manage to do both. Miranda Playfair, for instance,
who rejoined the band recently after a 20-year gap, plays on a modern American
instrument for the Academy and a period one for John Eliot Gardiner's *Orchestre
Révolutionnaire et Romantique.*

Although he made records with Thurston Dart demonstrating the Baroque style of playing – they did the Trio Sonatas of Purcell, for instance – Neville was never going to be part of the original-instrument crusade which developed in the 1970s. He was happy to play early music on modern instruments. This was not just because he wanted to secure the best players available, mostly to be found in symphony orchestras: he had – and still has – an aversion to any kind of dogma. The instruments of the Baroque period were less sophisticated and the strings less responsive, he says. 'I feel they just dry up the music.' And the prohibition of vibrato had been taken too far.

Neville finds the zeal of the so-called whole business irritating. 'As soon as musicians find they *can* make a better sound, they *want* to make a better sound. Beethoven wrote his five piano concertos when the fortepiano became the pianoforte – and he never went back to the fortepiano. You'd expect a composer to choose better instruments if he could get them.'

The contrast he has tried to make is with the heavy sound produced by players in Russia, and Central Europe – and hence in America where so many found refuge. Both in the strings and the wind, it is a richer, darker, more aggressive sound, which (as JB Priestley put it) made its way into the Anglo-Saxon world via Vienna and *gemütlichkeit*. 'We worked hard in the Academy to get the mud out of the texture,' Neville said.

But the differences are diminishing, because of what the conductor Robert Cole calls the 'globalization of style'. Even within the U.S. you used to be able to tell the Philadelphia symphony from the Cleveland, Boston from New York. The growing consensus, says Cole, is not necessarily a good thing.

The Academy's pursuit of transparency has been carried right through to the 19th century repertoire. But it doesn't work for all Romantic-age composers. 'I applied it to the Brahms symphonies,' Neville told me. 'Some of it worked wonderfully well, some of it rather weakened the texture.' He is more inclined nowadays to let orchestras have their way in this later music, while Ken Sillito as leader has sought to add a Romantic style of playing to the Academy's armoury. Neville remains shy of the high Romantic. 'Perhaps it's one of the weaker things of my concept of 19th century music; but I can't take Mahler and Bruckner seriously. I know it's a glorious noise, but quite often I can't follow their train of thought.' When playing modern music, starting with Stravinsky, the Academy's clean-cut style does, however, give it a head start over others.

Ditching the conductor: the democratic collective

A precedent was set, appropriately enough, in Bolshevik Russia where a group of players in Moscow, imbued with revolutionary fervour, got together in 1922 to form a conductorless symphony orchestra. They sat in a half circle with their backs to the audience. Similar experiments were made in the late 1920s in New York and Budapest.[4]

To achieve the kind of harmony required to make this work, you need musicians who are not only technically equipped, but who can co-operate closely, like a quartet does, and bring their own musical personalities to bear on the process.

In the beginning the Academy's string players were recruited from the front desks of symphony orchestras (Neville himself was principal second violin of the London Symphony Orchestra). And from the beginning, the best rates were paid, in order to get the best players. These days few have time to work both for the Academy and for symphonies, so generally play in other small ensembles.

The standard is very high. As Julia Fischer said during the US tour, you could almost swap the Academy players round, putting the front-deskers at the back and the back-deskers at the front, without making any difference. Someone might be playing at the back of the first violins for the Academy one day and leading a symphony orchestra the next.

Working without a conductor involves more than playing exactly in time and in tune, however. Chamber players, like members of string quartets, must be able to lead as well as to follow, to listen as well as to look, to contribute to the musical argument yet submerge their individuality to a musical consensus. And it is this process of finding consensus that rehearsals of the Academy are all about.

As we saw on the American tour, the technical *élan* of the orchestra strikes audiences wherever it goes. Even a seasoned musician like Ken Sillito was over-awed by his first experience of it. He used the well-worn motoring metaphor to describe his first day in the concert-master's chair: 'It was like sitting down in a Rolls-Royce and switching it on, and the Rolls-Royce took you through the Dvořák *Serenade* or whatever it was. The precision of the ensemble was terrifying. You can't use any other word for it.'

Robert Smissen, principal viola, who has played occasionally in many other bands told me: 'You are expected to perform in the Academy better than anywhere else. Neville always needed to see 'eyes up', not just following the part. And that continues.'

A family affair: Robert Smissen and his wife Rebecca Scott.

Photo: Christian Tyler

But first comes preparation. In the early days of the Academy, this was done by a democratic collective, even under the leadership of Neville. The small number of players, and the lack of deadlines, meant there was time to discuss every bar if necessary. Rehearsals could last for hours, even all night. Nor was there a fixed hierarchy in the band. Players would swap desks, and Neville would often ask other violinists to play the solos. As the orchestra grew in size, and began recording, there were too many people and too little time for protracted discussion. As time went on, democratic centralism – to borrow the phrase used in the Soviet Union – became the order of the day, with Neville cast in the role of 'benign dictator'.[5] Even today, as we saw on the Julia Fischer tour, the principals – and occasionally voices from further back – routinely have a hand in debating points of interpretation.

Decisions arrived at during rehearsal are marked into the parts by a player at each desk. Usually, it is the inside player who does this, putting in bowing marks for both (if strings); if it is a fingering, it is usual to check with the colleague first. When the band is under Ken Sillito's direction, without a guest director, it may be working from parts originally marked up by Neville and his colleagues many years before, at previous performances or for recordings. That is not to say they are cast in stone. Ken feels free to make what amendments he wants. And Neville himself will often change something he has come to regret.

[continued on page 42]

Translating the language of music

Debates about musical style reflect a deeper concern: the perennial problem of translating notes on paper into sound. There are difficulties here which even literate concertgoers, unless they are players themselves, tend to underestimate: they are not always aware how much more there is to performance than simply playing the notes. The translation must be a good one: it must be what the composer heard while putting the notes on paper.

Rehearsals are not for practising. Most players of Academy standard are instant sight-readers – indeed, British freelance musicians are famous for their skill at it. But if there is any note-learning to do, that happens in private practice before rehearsals begin. The point of rehearsal is to decide, in a phrase, 'how the music should go.'

Early composers left it almost entirely to performers to interpret the written notes, and to add ornamental flourishes. J.S. Bach, for instance, gives only a key-signature (C major, A minor, and so on), a time-signature, and a title ('Prelude', 'Fugue', 'Gavotte') but no indication of tempo, no dynamic markings (loud and soft, crescendo or diminuendo). Nor is there any indication of phrasing – how the notes should be grouped, and where the breaks, or breaths, should come. Later there would be a general indication of speed – from *largo* (very slow, literally 'broad') through *adagio* (literally 'at ease'), *andante* (literally 'going'), *allegretto* ('lively'), *allegro* ('very lively') to *presto* ('fast'). From the age of Beethoven onwards, composers' instructions became more and more copious until – in some modern scores – there are more composers' indications than there are notes. In John Cage's hands this reached a logical conclusion. His 1952 composition 4'33" for piano has only a composer's instruction, and no notes at all. Benjamin Britten, a very good conductor as well as a great composer, was famously sceptical about 'interpretation', at least when it came to his own music. 'I don't want people to interpret my music,' he told the conductor Sir Charles Mackerras. 'I want them to play it as written.' Even so, no composer can write down everything he intends: there just aren't the words or symbols – or the space – for it. In preparing Bartok's *Divertimento*, for example, Neville feels the need to put twice as many marks in the score as the composer has done.

Though it has a limited vocabulary, we can say that written music is a language. We can say also that it has 'meaning', even if it is hard to say what that meaning is. Of all the tasks which confront the conductor and performer – who are the interpreters, or translators of that language – phrasing is perhaps the most important. As Gerry Schwarz of the Seattle Symphony said: 'It is what music is all about.' By pressing down fingers and blowing down pipes, musicians turn symbols into sounds. But by interpreting or deciding 'how the music should go', especially by careful phrasing, they are giving those sounds a meaning.

To say that music has 'meaning' is not just to say that it is can sometimes be used to imitate nature: a piece which had nothing but cuckoo calls, rushing strings and rumbling drums would not become Beethoven's *Pastoral Symphony*. But to express this meaning in words is almost impossible. That is why chamber musicians often don't even attempt to explain to one another what they propose; they show it by playing it.

Leonardo da Vinci called music 'the shaping of the invisible'. Stravinsky, and many others, have compared it to architecture – an art which expresses itself by the combination and interplay of forms. Abstract painting is another popular analogy: the listener, like the viewer at an exhibition, is invited to admire and enjoy shapes and colours but is not expected to find a 'story' or representation behind them. Music has shape, of course, but sounds are also said to have 'colours': even on a mechanical instrument like the piano, a good player can produce different 'colours'. A nearer comparison might be with a foreign language, hearing someone give an impassioned speech in a language you do not know at all. There is rhetoric, emphasis, phrasing, gesticulation, smiles, perhaps tears – in other words, all manner of conveying meaning. You may have no clue to the sense and yet be moved by what you hear.

Musicians are not translating a foreign language, however, because although music has no 'sense', it contains familiar material: a distinct melody, or at least a motif or theme, harmonic progressions, and conventional endings of phrases or longer sections ('cadences') which are almost clichés. They are more like actors reading an obscure poem, or declaiming a difficult speech in a Shakespeare play. They learn the lines by heart, but at the same time they have to learn – usually with the help of the director – how to speak them. How fast is this line? Where is it loud, and where soft? Which words are to be emphasised? Should these lines run together, or does the sense require a break? Music has to be punctuated in just the same way. Every piece is a narrative in this sense, a song without words.

[continued from page 39]

The chamber orchestra 'standards' are kept by the Academy's librarian, Katherine Adams, at the orchestra's office in London's docklands. The symphonic music lives in 120 brown boxes on shelves at the top of the Marriners' house in South Kensington, where Molly keeps a card-index catalogue of the sort you found in public libraries before the PC age. This is the music Neville will use when he conducts the Academy 'big band', or one of his symphony orchestras abroad. Many conductors keep hold of orchestral parts as well as their own scores , and have them sent ahead when flying overseas. Similarly, soloist-directors like Julia Fischer, Joshua Bell and Julian Rachlin, when they are due to tour with the Academy, will either send their own sets of parts ahead of them or get the front desk parts scanned and transmitted to Katherine so that she can copy their marks into her set. Add up all the sets, including those marked up by Ken Sillito and former director Iona Brown, and you can see that the librarian's job is not as simple as it sounds. Katherine told me: 'I try not to keep stuff at home; there's no room. I spend my life heaving them around. I always have a car-full to take home and do work on. For the 'little band' there would be 10 volumes or more for a piece. But if you're playing five pieces in a concert, that's 50 – a suitcase load. A big symphony orchestra doing three different programmes on tour would have to take the parts round in a truck. On your US tour Nigel or Tara would have been carrying the parts in a suitcase: it's too risky to check them in.'

After preparation, execution. On the concert platform, the ability of the players to communicate is put to the severest test. 'You have to get inside each others' skin,' says Pauls Ezergailis.

What does this mean?

Sound travels slowly, much more slowly than light. In a big orchestra, it takes a fraction of a second for the sound to travel from the front to the back. The back players, therefore, will tend to fall behind. Not only that, but the back row will hear very little of what is going on up front – the din of brass, timpani and double basses will drown it out. For both these reasons, a symphony orchestra needs a conductor.

In a chamber orchestra, a conductor is dispensible if the players are good enough. You can see as well as hear. That means listening to where the lead is coming from – and it shifts around, according to the music. Unless everybody in the section is following the same lead, there will be confusion. But you still need to anticipate, to watch for visual signals. Every player acts as a 'beacon' to the one behind, lighting and then passing their beacon on: the front desk to the second row, the second to the third, and so on. At the same time, everyone must be able to see the leader: the movement of his bow or gestures he makes with his head. Players are like a rowing eight, where the timing of the crew as a whole is set by the one called 'stroke', but each oarsman moves in time with the man in front, and keeps his eye on the blade in front of his own, belonging to the man two seats ahead. And like a rowing eight, musicians must be perfectly together if they are to make any headway.

All this is done at the highest possible speed. And a player needs quick reactions. Cathy Elliott, one of the double bass players, tested hers at the Science Musem and discovered she had the same response time as a sprinter coming off the blocks at the starting gun. The trigger for a chamber player is the sight of a bow tip, or another player's gesture. At the same time they must allow for their own sound. If you can hear yourself (as a bass especially) you are probably too loud. This is a particular problem for wind players.

Dropping the conductor means extra responsibility for every section and for every player, which adds to the difficulty, but also to the enjoyment of making music. Many say that working under a conductor gives a 'second-hand feeling' because everyone is a split second away from the action – that is, the time it takes the signal from the conductor's baton to pass from the eye of the player to the brain and thence to the hand.

All this invokes the principle on which the orchestra was founded. Harvey de Souza made the point eloquently to a local reporter before the concert in Beaver Creek: 'Everybody participates; no-one sits around and just follows. We love it when we're in an intimate setting and can engage with the audience. In a small theatre, the audience can witness the incredible synergy of an ensemble playing without someone waving a stick at them. We live our lives through this music. We play as though our lives depend on it.'[6]

At what point does a conductor become necessary? It depends on the complexity of the music and to some extent on the acoustic of the hall. But these players, even at a strength of 40 or more, would be capable of delivering a Beethoven symphony without anybody waving from the podium. Indeed, they have done just that, performing Beethoven's Seventh under Joshua Bell. 'And it was electrifying,' says Harvey de Souza. In 2008, I watched them rehearse and perform Beethoven's *Emperor Concerto* with Barry Douglas directing from the piano – his first appearance with the Academy. The *Emperor* is normally considered too tricky to attempt without a conductor, Douglas told me. 'It needs a lot of organization. You need to be in control. Doing without a conductor solves a lot of problems but it creates problems too – about the ends of notes and phrases, for example. Because I'm in charge – but collaborating with the players – we can be much more together. The number one priority is to make sure that the soloist is comfortable.' I asked him how the Academy differed from other orchestras. 'What is different is that each of the players plays passionately, so you can hear that kind of vibrant musicality in a more transparent way than with symphony orchestras or more homogeneous ensembles.'

For symphonic players, the Academy offers not only a refuge from the conductor but a chance to make a mark. 'No player in this orchestra is afraid to be heard by himself or herself,' said Ken Sillito. 'And the other thing is, we all love music. That hasn't changed in 50 years.'

I was taken aback. 'You mean some players don't love music?'

'Yes. In symphony orchestras it can be just a job. Their children don't even know what Daddy does for a living. He leaves his fiddle in the car and never takes it out at home.' Ken Sillito's point is not fanciful. The conductor Mariss Jansons made exactly the same point when asked by *Gramophone* magazine to explain how he managed to get both his current orchestras into the magazine's list of the world's greatest (the Concertgebouw at No 1, the Bavarian Radio Symphony at No. 6). The musicians' love of music was the first thing he mentioned, along with a real desire to play in an orchestra, followed by a feeling of responsibility, hard work, and an utter lack of complacency. 'It sounds very strange, if you are talking about musicians [to say] they must like music. But believe me, it is not always the case. Music must be everything in your life.'

Musicians enjoy being able to move between bands. For the string players, as already noted, this generally means playing with other chamber ensembles. Wind and brass players, who are less often required, generally find it possible to combine Academy work with jobs at the big orchestras. If they are principals there, they will usually have a co-principal to stand in for them.

Some simply choose not to play in large orchestras, like Martin Humbey, a viola player with the Academy since the late 1980s, who was put off by a spell in the pit at Covent Garden. The Academy's flexibility is an attraction, therefore, says Simon Morris. 'There is a schedule for months ahead from which you can choose. And on every tour a slightly different group of people, so you don't get the cliqueyness that you get in symphonies, where people sit next to the same person all the time.'

Fitting in

But in a conductorless orchestra being good is not enough. Players have to fit in. As well as bringing their own musical personality they must be adaptable enough technically – and mentally – to play in the Academy style. They do this by listening, and by a process of osmosis. Young players may come in on a trial basis, and will be invited again only if they show they are quick enough to pass that test.

'If someone doesn't fit, they won't last. It becomes apparent quite quickly,' I was told by Catherine ('Katy') Jones, who has worked for the Academy for more than 30 years. Katy is the Academy's 'fixer': she books the players for concerts, drawing from the membership of about 50 players, and a pool of regular 'preferred extras' and new players from time to time. (The members are all freelance: membership gives preference, and some security, but no contract. They are booked separately for each and every bit of work.). Neville's summary was characteristically succint, explaining his recruitment method to the music writer Norman Lebrecht on Radio 3 in 2009: 'You could tell in two minutes whether they could play; later you would see if they fitted into the ensemble; then on tour to see if they were bearable.'

Typically, an Academy recruit is someone well able to play concertos when required, but who prefers to work in chamber music. Some have the technical skill to make it as a soloist on the international stage, but don't have the kind of

L to R:
Neville Marriner,
Alan Loveday and
Iona Brown.
Photo: Decca

temperament necessary, or are not prepared to endure the rigours of the life. Although every music college student is taught to play concertos and give recitals as if aiming for a solo career – this has been a matter of some contention – few aspire to it. Most apply in order to get the experience of playing in ensembles. Of all the quality fiddle players that have passed through the Academy, Neville mentions one in particular, the violinist Alan Loveday, as someone who could have had a solo career if he had chosen to. Iona Brown, Neville's successor as director of the chamber orchestra, did have a solo career; and Kenneth Sillito, the present director and former leader of the Gabrieli String Quartet, is another top-class player who might have done so. He told me that he never even felt inclined to try:

> 'I think there is something in the psyche, in the personality, that either pushes you to go on your own out there, or to be more interested in 'pure music'...Well, I shouldn't say that, but concertos are show pieces, not team work. For me really great music is the string quartet. It is the distillation of the finest of all composers' work, even if they only wrote one of them – like Ravel, Debussy, Verdi. These are masterpieces in their own right.'

In the old days, Academy players had no security of tenure. Neville was in charge of who played and who did not. 'Everyone was on the edge of their seat because they relied on that to be re-booked,' recalls Simon Morris. There were certain advantages to this regime. It discouraged a lot of the internal politics that goes with committee-run orchestras. 'For better or worse Neville made the decisions. The result was fantastic.' The maestro was always fussy. He said to me: 'If people are available, it means they're not so good. If they're really good, they're not available.' 'That may be true', counters Katy Jones, 'but you cannot get round it if you insist on having all the best players all the time.'

These days, a lot of younger people aim to get into the Academy as soon as possible after college, and use that in order to win jobs as principals in full-time orchestras. 'It's the best thing to have on your CV now', says Neville, somewhat crossly. 'Sometimes they do not even realize that it's only a part-time orchestra.'

Young musicians often form quartets and other ensembles of their own; and if the Academy has one of the players on its books, it tries to involve the others too – it makes life easier for both parties. The Emperor Quartet all play for the Academy: Martin Burgess, Clare Hayes, Fiona Bonds and Will Schofield, are a successful group nominated for a Grammy award for their recording of the Walton String Quartet. Ken Sillito, Robert Smissen and Stephen Orton make up three quarters of the Pro Arte piano quartet. And when one of the women of the Barbirolli Quartet – known as the 'Barbies' – became a regular extra, her colleagues were auditioned too. In the past Malcolm Latchem, Colin Sauer and Michael Evans were in the Dartington Quartet, playing and teaching at the famous music college of that name in Devon. And there were players from no fewer than four quartets in the orchestra when the Academy recorded the Strauss *Metamorphosen* in 1968.

Players were recruited by word of mouth in the old days, and sometimes almost on impulse. Malcolm Latchem was tipped off while sharing a taxi with a cellist in Edinburgh after a concert with the RPO. 'The cellist said: "Neville's looking for one more violin for a Baroque orchestra". Neville had heard me play one evening three years earlier when Alan Loveday brought him round: he had to listen to me do the first movement of the Bartok sonata for solo violin. He was very patient. And he said Yes. I went in as the third 2nd violin.'

Ken Sillito tells how one night in the late 1970s, after a concert with his quartet and on his way back North, he stopped for a mug of tea at Jack's Hill Café on the old A1 outside Stevenage. 'A chap came up to me still in his tails and said 'Hello, Ken! Why don't you join the Academy?' It was Neville, of course, in the inimitable Neville style, just having done an Academy date somewhere. He planted the seed in my mind.' Ken did not actually join until 1980 after being approached by Malcolm Latchem who was looking for someone to direct the chamber ensemble (then usually known as 'The Octet').

Later, there were auditions, but not every newcomer was obliged to sit for one. Wind players, for example, were already known and were chosen for their reputation.

The cellist John Heley, who joined in the mid-1980s, told me it had been his ambition to play for the Academy since he was 14, when his father brought home a record called *The World of the Academy, Volume Two*). Miya Ichinose, who is

Malcolm Latchem.
Photo: Decca

on the 'preferred extras' list, knew the Academy from its soundtrack of the film *Amadeus,* which came out when she was a child, and heard her parents – both professional string players – talk about it. She got in on the recommendation of a family friend. She plays with the second violins of the LSO, but on the Julia Fischer tour of the U.S. she was sitting with the firsts; she had never experienced a conductorless orchestra before.

A remarkable recent recruit is Samson Diamond, a young black South African violinist from Soweto township who e-mailed Katy Jones from Manchester. Intrigued by his CV, which revealed that he had been leader of the 'Buskaid Soweto String Ensemble' and was playing for the Hallé orchestra, she rang him back to say there was an audition a week later. Someone had dropped out and he could take their place:

'He rang back an hour later and said: 'I realize it's crazy at such short notice, but I'm going to do it.' He got to the audition about an hour and a half early, freezing cold in the chilly hall and shaking like a leaf. It was the end of a long evening and we thought: 'here's a real no-hoper, an unknown.' But then he played, and everyone went 'Wow!' He played Mozart beautifully, and a piece he'd dug out of the library of the Royal Northern College of Music for his finals. He was inexperienced and had a lot to learn, but he really performed, he really delivered. And so he went on the extras list for dates with the "big band". So you never know…'

I met Samson at London's Henry Wood Hall in January 2009 during rehearsals for the big band's upcoming tour to Germany and Austria. He had been featured in the *Readers Digest* a month before, he told me. I asked him what he thought of his new role. 'It's the most vitalising musical experience you can have on stage,' he said. 'It's a different level of commitment. You feel completely liberated as a string player. You feel 'This is why I love playing music.''

John Heley waiting to face the Chardstock fast bowlers. *Photo: Christian Tyler*

Family matters

I wrote at the beginning of this chapter that a successful chamber orchestra needs four things: good players, good teamwork, good ears and a strong ethos or *ésprit de corps*. For members of the Academy of St. Martin in the Fields, the last ingredient came from a strong sense of belonging to one family.

Julian Rachlin, quoted earlier in this chapter, used the family metaphor unprompted. It is particularly apt. Neville and Molly Marriner have been like parents to this group of musicians, or – since we are beginning to see a third generation of players in the orchestra – grandparents. Even when Neville stepped back to pursue a separate career, the Academy did not stop being a family affair.

The bond of family matters for musicians, just as it is does for soldiers. Regiments in the British Army (unlike those of other nations) cultivate this sense of identity, taking recruits from the same towns or counties, and from successive generations of the same families. Like soldiers, musicians train together, spend a lot of time in each other's company, and go into battle together. Above all, each depends completely on his fellow: If they don't stick absolutely together, they are lost.

A recent BBC television film about the Berlin Philharmonic on tour in China suggested a deeper psychological factor. Some of the players talked of lonely childhoods, not being quite accepted by other children, or regarded by their own families as a little odd. A young woman told the camera that the way she talked to others was through her French horn. An oboist who stuttered could be fluent only with music. New arrivals were like adopted children coming into a big family, according to Simon Rattle, current chief conductor of the Berlin Phil. Would they fit, or not? A player said it was not always easy to belong: the bigger the group, the more difficult. A former manager of the LSO, Clive Gillinson, the cellist who saved the orchestra from financial collapse in the 1980s,

Tristan Fry, the Academy's timpanist: 'a lovely feeling of cohesiveness right to the back'
Photo: Christian Tyler

always talked of it as a family: not only the players, but patrons, sponsors and office staff, even the star soloists like Rostropovitch and Boulez. It was his way of establishing a new ethos.[7]

The Academy's solidarity is not so all-embracing. But it is strong among the players, not merely the 'core' string players or those occupying the front desks, but all the way back to the timpanist. 'It's my home: a family,' said Tristan Fry, who has been principal timpanist for 40 years. 'I was at a very impressionable age, 18 or 19, when I started. It was in the mid-60s, and percussion had become quite a big thing in those days – Boulez, Stockhausen and so on.' He had played with the John Dankworth band, with a group led by John Williams called 'Sky', and was the session drummer for all the James Bond films and some of the *Pink Panther* and *Harry Potter* series. 'Instead of being just a crasher and banger at the back I was playing with the Academy those wonderful authentic pieces. That gave you a sort of balance, feet on the ground of music. That's why I say it's home – like going back to your Mum and Dad.'

Probably because of its origins as a small string band, he added, the orchestra created a 'lovely feeling of cohesiveness which stretches back to me, even though I'm furthest away both musically and in distance. Apart from listening, you have to physically see each other to get a feeling of how we're all thinking. I find this beautiful relationship with the string players which you rarely get anywhere else.'

It is a family, but a freelance one. The Academy may be 'home', but the freedom to play away seems to be essential. Just as in real families, people behave better when not on top of each other all the time. Indeed, for family get-togethers they are expected to be at their best. Matthew Ward says:

> 'What I've noticed is a kind of innate trust that there will be this level of ex-cellence. You can go to another orchestra and see many of the same players, but there is something missing, because the expectation is not there. It's about attitude and a common joy in music-making, about being fit in all aspects: as a player, as a musician with a creative mind – without sounding too grandiose about it – and playing as an artist in your own right because it's you, and not just a name off a list.'

Schools, hospitals, university colleges, newspapers: all strive to create some sort of family atmosphere, to preserve a distinct ethos. So of course do sporting teams, where on the football field or cricket pitch loyalty is as valued as on the front line of battle. The secrets of successful leadership are studied almost obses-sively. Let us take an example from cricket (the game which is Neville Marriner's private passion and therefore in a sense the 'house sport' of the Academy): a former captain of Middlesex declared in a recent radio interview that in a team, individuality should be nurtured. The tendency in professional sport, influenced by management jargon, was to try and smooth out differences. That was all wrong. Let the captain create a 'culture of non-interference', he said, because enthusiasm was everything.

Orchestras have been used as a management training device. In one scheme, called 'The Music Paradigm', senior managers are dotted about the orchestra like students on work experience in order to feel how each section responds to the others. They are taken to stand behind the conductor's podium (or even allowed to conduct) in order to feel the power at the conductor's disposal, the force of all the sections combining at the focal point. Some of the big names of American in-dustry have endorsed this model of how different divisions of a company can be made to pull together for the boss.[8] An even more ambitious use of the orchestra as metaphor is Daniel Barenboim's West-Eastern Divan Orchestra, which brings together young Israelis, Palestinians and other Arabs in order to teach mutual understanding, tolerance and a sense of inter-dependence.[9]

Vikram Seth, at the beginning of his novel about a string quartet, *An Equal Music*, describes the quartet as 'a quadripartite marriage with six relationships.' How many more relationships, then, in a chamber orchestra of 21 or a small symphony orchestra of 40? The bonds formed in making music can easily become emotional ties: even more than actors, who usually meet only temporarily, musicians are thrown together in their own peculiar world for years on end. Not surprisingly, they sometimes become lovers, and marry each other. This can work well – both partners know the score – but it can also create tensions.

The life of a professional musician makes high emotional as well as physical and psychological demands, and that is something only another musician understands. The Academy's principal horn player, Tim Brown, a highly-regarded soloist and a man of wide interests, thinks that music creates ideals of perfection. 'It's an idealised world, which real life doesn't often mirror. So a real life relationship may disappoint. It's an ideal world into which one can retreat.' Only those who are emotionally mature can cope with the rigours of touring: only they can cope with the high level of emotional commitment required by the music, as well as the hunger, tiredness and loneliness (which can lead the innocent into liaisons that later cause embarrassment).

The Academy likes to think of itself as enjoying the communicative intimacy of the string quartet. Vikram Seth, in the book already quoted, was not sure whether to compare it with a marriage, a business, a platoon under fire, or a 'self-regarding, self-destructive priesthood' which had 'so many tensions mixed in with its pleasures'.[10]

Now it is true that some string quartets have survived for years with members not on speaking terms, like the famous quartet whose members always stayed in different hotels and travelled in different cars. Music somehow overrides personal antipathy. But this is not always so. In a sensitive organism like a chamber orchestra, any strain between players, especially when it involves partners or married couples – or divorced couples – is quickly felt by the rest of the collective. In general, outbursts of temper, which can occur at the end of a long tour, are easily defused because of the mutual respect which the players have for each other. But if personalities are in constant clash, the effects can be painful and far-reaching, as we shall see later in the book.

One person who does a lot to maintain harmony within the band is the 'fixer'. Katy Jones probably knows the Academy players better than anybody: they confide in her if they are having domestic problems. It is a job which requires the tact to keep players happy with the firmness to make sure they turn up when required.

Katy says her job is regarded as the hardest of all, because you can only get it wrong. She has stuck with it, she says, because she loves the people she deals with. 'You have to understand the dynamics, where others just see a list of names.' The fixer has to find the right balance of players, by temperament and experience, especially in the strings. In some cases, sharing a desk creates a bond; in others it leads to trouble. Little things can create big resentments:

> 'One player on a desk may complain of feeling evil glances from the other. A fiddle player rang me up once before a tour and said 'there's a good chance I may share a desk with (so and so) , and please can you prevent that? '. I asked why. Because, she said, last time she leaned over and criticized me: 'I think you need to give a bit more bow here…' No-one has the right to do that. And the next comment was: 'is that your *best* bow?' Others who are regarded as difficult you can find a partner for. Women are often good at that. They say: 'I don't mind playing next to so and so, because I can manage them.'

Leaving the family

If music is your life, and the orchestra is like your family, leaving it can be a terrible prospect. Musicians age, like everyone else, but their decline occurs at different rates. There is no official retirement age, and no target for what the average age of the members should be, although the policy is to try and keep a balance of experienced players and newcomers. It all comes down to how well players are performing. Having to tell someone that he or she is going off the boil is the worst job there is.

When Neville Marriner was in charge, he was the one who did it. It cannot have been easy, but his pursuit of perfection trumped all other considerations:

> 'When it came to firing people I had to do it, in as friendly way as I could. Because no one in the orchestra was going to tell them. You only need one principal player to be not good enough for the whole standard of performance to go. It doesn't *start* to go, it *goes*. You can't go on repeating things just because someone can't play it. And as soon as one or two can' t meet the standard, record companies and the public notice, and the critics. And then it's very hard to persuade people you are competent. It's like an actor with a speech impediment. To keep the group alive economically you have to accept these things. Good relations are important, but they're not the first priority.'

If this sounds harsh, it must be recorded that Neville can be just as hard on himself. He likes to say he gave up leading the Academy when he realised he had become the kind of violinist he would never recruit into the orchestra. As often with Neville, it is not easy to tell how much of this is joking: others say he was a much better violinist than he pretends.

When everyone knew it was Neville's decision, parting was painful but usually simple. Neville would instruct Katy Jones not to book so-and-so again, and take the consequences (Players joke that he sometimes managed to be away when the blow fell.) But, as in other areas of the band's operations, even when Neville gave up formal control, players continued to assume he was still calling the shots, even when he was not.

There are always sighs of relief when players step down voluntarily. Some ask to be warned as soon as doubts are voiced about their peformance. The inevitable decline that comes with age can be accommodated by principals giving up their front desk and going back to the ranks. Parting can even be painless. When Dawn Day was general manager she rang a wind player who had continued into his 70s. He asked if she was ringing about his retirement. 'Well, actually, yes,' replied Dawn. 'He did a couple more concerts that he wanted to do, and left,' she recalled. 'It was all very amicable.'

Some players remain confident, says Katy, but others can become very insecure, even in repertoire they have played a thousand times. 'It's all very, very hard,' she added. 'People ask: "why don't you issue a warning?". But this is somebody's whole life.' The management had become better at handling retirement, she added, but still occasionally got it wrong.

The present system is that if players, directors or conductors are concerned about an individual's performance, the question is raised at a meeting of the principals. Wider opinons will be sought and, if there is consensus that something has to be done, the next step is to speak to the player concerned.

The Marriners know what it is to lose a treasured player. In the summer of 2008, their own son Andrew, the Academy's virtuoso clarinettist, had to give up his membership. His work as principal clarinet of the LSO was taking up so much time that the Academy rarely saw him. At the same time the principal flautist Jaime Martin, another fine soloist, had to leave for the same reason.

Chapter Three

EARLY DAYS

THE name was always a problem. Appropriate though it was to the circumstances of its birth, 'The Academy of St Martin-in-the-Fields' was a mouthful: cumbersome, confusing, difficult to abbreviate, and a challenge to graphic designers. The hyphens alone were a nuisance, and were later dropped.

'It took me years to remember the Academy's full name correctly,' wrote Alfred Brendel, who knew the orchestra well. 'A group with such an impossible name had either to be dreary, or become a legend. It became the latter...'[1]

In Asia, keen young music students would queue up after concerts to ask how they might apply 'to study at your academy.' Americans, like the man in the audience in Mesa, Arizona, who was relieved to discover the orchestra had not been founded in the open countryside, had special difficulty with it. The music critic of the *Berkshire Eagle* thought it might be a typical British joke – something out of Monty Python, perhaps. A Californian commuter, constantly hearing the radio announcement 'Neville Marriner conducting the Academy of St. Martin in the Fields,' wrote, tongue in cheek, to his local paper:

The famous parrot cartoon which says it all.
Charles Rodrigues/Stereo Review

'Why must he conduct in the fields? What kind of sadist is this Neville Marriner? Dragging those kids and their heavy instruments outside in that God-awful English weather and expecting them to play their hearts out. I must confess that the boys and girls of St Martin's do a bang-up job, but the sound of that chill wind roaring off the heath in the background sends shivers up and down my steering-column.'[2]

The name was actually suggested by Michael Bowie, the viola player who was in at the very start. The word 'Academy' referred back not to Plato in ancient Athens, but to the title often adopted by European musical societies in the 17th and 18th centuries. As for the rest of the name, it was taken in homage to the church where the orchestra was conceived and first played in public, a fine neo-classical edifice by James Gibbs with pedimented portico and tiered spire, which dominates the eastern side of Trafalgar Square in London.

Gibbs's building had replaced an old church which had indeed once stood 'in the fields' – but had not done so since the late 1500s. Dedicated to Saint Martin of Tours, the fourth-century bishop who cut his cloak to clothe a shivering beggar, St Martin-in-the-Fields (complete with hyphens, like so many London

The church of St Martin-in-the-Fields, a sketch by Kenneth Heath, a founder member of the Academy.

churches) became the parish church of Buckingham Palace, half a mile away down the Mall. On its completion in 1726 King George I was made churchwarden and donated a fine organ, which may have been played by Handel himself.

In the Spring of 1958, John Churchill, master of music at St. Martin's, and Michael Bowie, a former pupil of his, agreed that what the church needed was a professional orchestra to replace the church's now defunct chamber group.[3] Bowie had played in that group, and was now assistant principal at the LSO. He approached Norman Nelson, a violinist who had joined the LSO at the same time as him, and Simon Streatfeild, who as principal viola occupied the same desk at the LSO as Bowie.

Having got the support of the vicar, the Rev. Austen Williams, and of the church's music committee, the four men repaired to a pub behind St Martin's to

Kenneth Heath, principal cellist from the beginning until his death in 1977.

thrash out a plan over pints of ale. They quickly agreed on who should be leader: an energetic and self-confident 33-year-old who was also at the LSO as principal second violin, by the name of Neville Marriner.

Neville was an obvious choice. Not only was he used to commanding a section of string players, he had played a lot of chamber music before joining the LSO. Through his friendship with Thurston Dart, he knew the late Baroque period, the 'golden age of string music', which the group was going to make its speciality. The period was roughly 1680-1750, the lifetimes of Bach and Handel, which saw the development of the *concerto grosso* in Italy. The music was, of course, entirely appropriate to the date (not to mention the acoustic) of the church itself.

Simon Streatfeild recalls that once Neville had been chosen, the rest of the time was spent tossing around names of prospective members. They had in mind a 12-piece band: six violins, two violas, two cellos, a double bass, and continuo, a part which fell naturally to church organist John Churchill. Funds for the venture came from a £1,000 donation by the Pilgrim Trust.

The first line-up looked like this: Neville Marriner, Norman Nelson and Raymond Keenlyside (first violins); Malcolm Latchem, Anthony Howard and Tessa Robbins (second violins); Simon Streatfeild and Michael Bowie (violas); Wilfred Simenauer and Kenneth Heath (cellos); John Gray (double bass); and John Churchill on the harpsichord.

From the beginning the idea was to play as much as possible in the format and style of the Baroque. In an early mission statement, Michael Bowie declared that there was to be rigorous discipline and 'no wandering into other styles'. He wrote:

Once the rot sets in it is impossible to retain any identity for the ensemble . . .
The group becomes just another of those bands that play every sort of music.
The Academy of St Martin-in-the-Fields is not interested in joining their ranks.[4]

(Twenty years later Bowie noted that he had been a little idealistic. The band had been compelled to make itself more marketable, and its repertoire changed accordingly.)

The climate was absolutely right for the venture. 'Early music', as the Baroque was called, was enjoying one of its many revivals, so the Academy was surfing the wave that it was itself helping to create. Just as important, stereo LPs had recently arrived on the market, allowing listeners to enjoy the kind of precision and clarity which were to become the Academy's hallmark.

Preparation of the music was meticulous, and scholarly. Michael Bowie, later helped by Denis Stevens, researched the scores and marked up the parts. He was helped by his discovery of the *Essay on Musical Expression* by Charles Avison, an English pupil of Francesco Geminiani, who in turn was a pupil of Corelli, one of the masters of the Italian Baroque. He also found, in the British Museum, Avison's *Concerto in A major* from 1766, which the Academy revived and later recorded. The concerto was the great invention of the period. Corelli left a set of twelve *Concerti Grossi* which Michael Bowie described as 'perfect examples of the Baroque style in its purest form.' The most beautiful, and a favourite of the band, was his *Op. 6, No. 3* in C minor.

As for the style of playing, clues were to be found in Geminiani's *The Art of Playing on the Violin* (1751), and from him the Academy learned to play with all the bows moving in the same direction, up or down. 'We used to play everything from the string, at the line of least resistance, where it all felt most comfortable,' explained Neville. 'That way you didn't get a harsh attack.'

John Churchill, who had studied continuo playing from works such as F.T. Arnold's *The Art of Accompaniment from a Thorough-Bass*, compiled from instructions of the period, kept the ensemble together on continuo, a harpsichord lent by the famous maker Thomas Goff.

St Martin's church was not a good place to rehearse. The main body of the church was always busy, with people coming in and out, while the crypt in those days was a too clutered. Trafalgar Square with the National Gallery on one side, Nelson's column in the middle with its four monumental Landseer lions and its fountains and pigeons, was a tourist Mecca; and there was nowhere to park.

So the players met in the Marriners' flat off Gloucester Road in South Kensington. They would arrive after rehearsing with their own orchestras, and depart in time for their evening concerts. Or they would come after work, and play far into the night. It was a bit of a crush at the flat, especially when the band expanded to tackle something like a Brandenburg Concerto. Up to 20 players would be crammed into the sitting room, Molly recalls, with a horn player warming up in the main bedroom and another wind player squawking in their daughter's room. All but two of the players were smokers; the fug can be imagined. Molly found herself having to hump the music stands about in their heavy bags, and fetching music parts from where they were stored. Later, the Academy used the premises of the British Institute of Recorded Sound not far away in Exhibition Road. (This became the National Sound Archive, which moved eventually to the British Library.)

The democratic procedures of the Academy meant that they all worked out the bowings and everyone had a say in how the the music should go. Later, Neville began to mark up all the parts himself, which reduced the amount of discussion. He did it himself because marking the score and giving it to a copyist to transfer to the parts somehow failed to produce the sound he was after. 'It's quite ridiculous, I know, but there seems to be something in a way you actually put it down on paper that convinces the player.'[5] Norman Nelson recalled: 'Once I grumbled to Nev about a marking, and Nev said "Do the bloody things yourself!".'

Surrounded by players who were themselves leaders, Neville had no choice but to be collegiate.[6] All had their say in rehearsal, even if some were more vocal than others, and music was chosen to give leading players a prominent role, individually or in groups. Yet as a leader of leaders, Neville was able to achieve a homogeneity of style, more by demonstrating than by talking. John Gray the bass player described it: 'He was able to turn round and say "No. Try a faster bow stroke, further away from the bridge; *this* part of the bow; *this* sort of sound."'

The first concerts, beginning in the autumn of 1958, were a series of five try-outs, to iron the kinks out of performance and test public response to 'early music'. Not many people turned up to listen to them that winter, but by the end a good review had appeared in *The Times* and the BBC had asked to record half an hour of Albicastro, Corelli and Handel.

The first 'professional' concert took place on Friday 13th November 1959, the

date which the Academy considers its true birthday. Announced as the first of a series called 'A survey of the Baroque Concerto', it featured Albinoni, Torelli, Corelli and Locatelli, some of that clutch of composers irreverently dubbed 'the Italian ice-cream merchants'. Denis Stevens supplied a programme note on the origin of the concerto. A postcript added: 'During a short interval after the third item, a silver collection will be taken to pay the expenses of this concert.'[7]

By now the Pilgrim Trust donation was running out, and five of the musicians recombined under the name 'The Ambrosian Players' to broadcast for the BBC from country houses. A gig at Hampton Court Palace nearly collapsed when they forgot to book a harpsichordist. Overhearing their problem, a man who was looking round the pictures said he could play the harpsichord a bit. He saved the broadcast.

It was a difficult start. After the first series of concerts, very little time was spent at St Martin's. A recital with George Malcolm at the Wigmore Hall did not repay the cost of mounting it, and a freezing cold tour of Ireland nearly brought the whole venture to an end.

For this tour half the band had taken leave from their day jobs with the LSO, where five of them were front-desk players. They had been allowed to go on the strict understanding they were back in time to join the LSO's upcoming tour to Israel. It was a tight call: there were only four hours between the time of their scheduled arrival at Heathrow airport from Dublin, and the LSO's departure

*[continued on
page 64]*

The Young Marriner

If the Academy chose an inauspicious day for its first professional concert, a Friday the 13th, its new director's choice of birthday was hardly less so. The young Marriner was born on April 15, 1924, twelve years to the day after the sinking of the *Titanic*. His birthplace was the cathedral city of Lincoln, where nothing much had happened musically since William Byrd was taken on as organist and choir-master in 1562.

It was his father, Herbert, who introduced Neville to the violin at the age of five. A carpenter and builder, he was a musician *manqué* who played the piano for church services, conducted chapel choirs and an annual performance of the *Messiah*, and had also taken a few lessons from a violin-playing artist, as payment for posing for her. Neville's mother Ethel had a good voice. There was a lot of music in the house.

Marriner Senior did not think music a suitable career for a boy, however. He was put off by the sight of the impoverished players of the Hallé orchestra misbehaving on the seafront at Scarborough where the family took its summer holidays. Yet he was keen to see what young Neville could do, and when it turned out that the boy had talent, he entered him for local festivals in Lincoln and neighbouring towns.

'I usually managed to win something,' Neville says modestly. But in a place like Lincoln, he was something of a sensation. When at the age of 13 he won the Open Class in a competition against all comers, the professor of the Royal College of Music who was judging said he should go to London for an audition.

Three years later he was admitted to the RCM on a scholarship, having left the local grammar school. He was taught first by W.H. ('Willy') Read, a close friend of Elgar's, and later by Albert Sammons, whom he regards as the most distinguished English violinist of that time – and who was also Elgar's preferred performer for his Violin Concerto. At the RCM Neville won the Tagore Gold Medal for the most distinguished student contribution to college life (an award that in later life he rarely mentioned).

After the war he returned to the RCM, graduated, and became a professor there. He went to the Paris Conservatoire for nearly a year to study under René Benedetti, and came back sounding quite different (though how much was due to Benedetti is not clear). He taught for a year at Eton College, where he had the awkward job of advising the mother of George Christie, the future inheritor of Glyndebourne, whether the boy should become a professional musician.

His first chamber group was a trio, started in 1949 with the violinist Alan Loveday and the pianist Antony Hopkins to play Baroque and some modern music. With Thurston Dart he formed the Jacobean Ensemble to concentrate on the Baroque; there he met the cellist Denis Vigay who remembers him as 'a bit of a joker in a canary-coloured waistcoat and a perky manner.' He also played second violin in the Martin String Quartet. Later came the Virtuoso Trio, with Alexander Kok and Stephen Shingles, the viola player who was to be the Academy's long-serving principal. All the while he was teaching at the RCM and working freelance with London symphony orchestras, settling at the LSO in 1956 as principal second violin, a job he did not give up until 1969 when his conducting career began.

When the new orchestra of the Academy of St Martin in the Fields found a leader, it also acquired a manager. Neville had just married his second wife, Elizabeth

Sims – always and to this day known as 'Molly' – an Oxford graduate whose grip on practical matters was as great as her love of literature. As it happens, they were introduced by Neville's small daughter, Susie, who, with her infant brother Andrew was living in a house in Brook Green, Hammersmith. Neville shared the house with John Amis, a friend of Molly's from Oxford. And when Molly came to visit him in Neville's absence, she and Susie quickly became friends. On one of her subsequent visits to see Susie, it was Neville who opened the door.

[continued from page 61]

from Gatwick to Tel Aviv. Molly Marriner arranged a mini-bus to take them from one to the other. When they got to Dublin, however, they learned that the airport fuel-loaders had gone on strike and the flight would be delayed – by four hours. Fearful of the consequences not only for the future of their new chamber group but for their jobs, they made a desperate early morning phone call to the LSO manager. Hardly had the explanations begun before they learned that divine intervention had saved them. Dense fog at Gatwick had grounded all the planes.[8]

Financial salvation came from the market, for the new stereo LPs were appearing. It was decided to make an audition tape to play to the record companies. With the help of Jimmy Burnett, a technician friend at the BBC, a Handel *Concerto Grosso* was recorded in the church at two o'clock in the morning when the traffic in Trafalgar Square was at its quietest. Neville was made responsible for hawking the tape round London.

The Lyre-bird

Neville believes that you make your own luck. And his long career has consequently been blessed by serendipity. The serendipitous event that now occurred was one of the most important.

By coincidence, the first record company that Neville approached knew Jimmy Burnett who had helped make the tape, and they asked his opinion of it. Burnett was able to say, truthfully, that he thought the Academy were terrific, and recommended that the company make a series of six records. The company was *L'Oiseau-Lyre* – 'the lyre bird' – and its owner was an Australian heiress interested in unusual music and unknown artists. She was Louise Dyer (her company's name contains echoes of her own), born in Melbourne and trained as a pianist and singer, taking a few lessons from Dame Nellie Melba herself. Arriving in Europe in 1927, she founded a music publishing company in Paris, Lyre-Bird Press, but lived half the time in Monte Carlo.

In March 1961, the players sat down in the Conway Hall, Red Lion Square, to record 'A Recital by the Academy of St Martin-in-the-Fields' consisting of the usual suspects: Corelli, Albicastro, Torelli, Locatelli, and Handel. There were no royalties for this; Mrs Dyer paid the musicians up front, a fiver each extracted from a big white leather bag.

Mrs Dyer sat in the control box looking at her watch while the Academy did 40 minutes of music in two sessions. There was an unplanned break when

STEREO SOL 60045   RECITAL by ACADEMY OF ST. MARTIN-IN-THE-FIELDS

A RECITAL
by THE ACADEMY of
ST MARTIN-IN-THE-FIELDS
DIRECTED by
NEVILLE MARRINER

first record, for
L'Oiseau–Lyre.

Neville rushed out to buy gut E strings for the fiddles because the modern ones sounded too shrill in the hall. Burnett the producer described the scene as hair-raising and frenetic: 'Neville was sweating on the top line; there was no let-up whatso-ever and not one fraction of a second was wasted.'[9]

As well as being clever, determined and rich, the proprietor of *L'Oiseau-Lyre* was thrifty. 'She was rather formidable,' said one player, 'and the rest of us left Neville to look after her.' She travelled second-class and couldn't bear to pay for overtime. Perhaps she was partly resonsible for making Neville so efficient at recording, the basis of the orchestra's future fame and fortune. Their 'Recital' was given a golden notice in *Gramophone*, where it was described as 'played with precision, care, consummate musicianship, and with more sense of style than all the other chamber orchestras in Europe put together.'

A second 'Recital' followed in 1963, with Avison, Manfredini, Albinoni, Handel and Telemann on the label. *Stereo Review* raved: 'aurally one of the most stunning groups of its kind… the second volume is every bit as good as the first.' Edward Greenfield wrote in *The Guardian* that the Academy was set to become the leading chamber group in the country.

Mrs Dyer had died in 1962, and although more records were to be made with *L'Oiseau –Lyre*, the Academy was now taken up by Argo, another small company, started by Harley Usill with a friend of his in 1950 almost as a hobby and aimed at the new market for the spoken word. Argo had since become part of Decca, and had moved into music. Harley (a cricket fan and decent swing bowler) of-fered to record Handel's *Op.3 concerti* for wind and strings, and in 1965 was given an exclusive five-year contract – exclusive, that is, but for *L'Oiseau-Lyre*, to which the players wished to show their gratitude.

The contract brought work at Cambridge. A long series of recordings with St John's College choir under George Guest began in 1964 with anthems by Purcell, and continued into the late 1970s. It included a set of Haydn Masses which Prime Minister Edward Heath later presented to Pope Paul VI on a visit to the Vatican in 1972. One of the soloists for these Argo discs was the young tenor Robert Tear, beginning a career-long association with the Academy.

A no less fruitful partnership was established at the other end of Trinity Street at King's College Chapel, with the rival – and more famous – choir under Sir David Willcocks. Twelve recordings were made here from 1965, in one of England's most inspired religious buildings.

For these sessions the continuo was provided by resident organ scholars, including Andrew Davis and Simon Preston who went on to work with the Academy. Neville led the orchestra, and in the front of the choir stood a small boy, his son Andrew, who had just passed his audition after the following exchange of courtesies:

Sir David Willcocks: 'And how old are you, Andrew?'

Andrew: 'Eight, sir. How old are you?'

Andrew was the catalyst for one of the Marriners' longest friendships. In a letter home from choir school he mentioned a 'nice man' in the choir. Molly suggested that on her next visit to Cambridge the 'nice man' be invited to tea at the Blue Boar. The man turned out to be Brian Kay, an 18-year-old King's choral scholar and founder member of what became The King's Singers, a group which Neville later helped make famous. As it happened, Brian Kay had rooms on the same staircase as E.M.Forster; so Molly, whose degree was in English literature, invited him to tea as well. Brian Kay went on to be a well-known BBC radio presenter and choral conductor.

The choristers were encouraged to make a bright 'Italian' sound to match the Academy's own. The trouble was that the trebles, especially the youngest ones, tended to give their all on the first take of the recording while the orchestra was just warming up, and then relapse into boredom for the endless re-takes. Willcocks tried the trick of under-rehearsing them to keep them alert; but they learned to save themselves for the second take instead. King's College Chapel has a notoriously difficult acoustic, which visiting musicians find hard to handle: chords take seven seconds to die, the echo comes back flat, and every bad sound is magnified. (I remember it defeating Yehudi Menuhin, when I heard him play Bach solo violin sonatas there in the early 1960s.) The place is cold, too. Principal cellist Kenneth Heath wore mittens and carried a hip flask; Celia Nicklin, the principal oboist, found herself filling hot-water-bottes for the visiting soloists Elly Ameling, Dietrich Fischer-Dieskau and Dame Janet Baker.

Janet Baker remembered these early recordings as 'joyous':

'The Academy had an enthusiasm one didn't often find among professional orchestras, and the choir was full of young singers eager to enter the profession; you'd hear this marvellous obbligato playing starting up behind you in this superb building, and it would all take off like a jet aeroplane.'[10]

Brian Kay also remembered those Cambridge days with pleasure: the pub

Time off: the path
from Dartington
down to the Cott Inn.

Photo: KIPPA

crawls, the expeditions, and climbing back into college when the gates were locked at midnight. The Academy was not like other bands, he said. It was a handful of people 'having the time of their lives.' Like the King's Singers it had 'that desire to get away from the conductor's baton and to form an ensemble which thrived on internal combustion.'[11]

Public appearances were still rare. Festival concerts were a chance for the Academy to show itself to British audiences. York was first, in 1963, with the soprano Heather Harper and horn player Barry Tuckwell. Then followed Harrogate, Bath, King's Lynn, Edinburgh, Chichester and Norwich. These were celebrity events in which the Academy backed big-name soloists like Heinz Holliger, Jean-Pierre Rampal, Josef Suk, Ileana Cotrubas and Fou Ts'ong. (Years later that would become the standard format of the chamber orchestra's tours).

Music while you play

Every summer for seven years, from 1964 to 1970, the band went on a busman's holiday to Dartington Hall, in Devon, to rehearse, give concerts for music students, and have fun.

A 14th-century palace with a Great Hall and vast kitchen, tilting yard, lawns, terraced gardens and thousand-year-old yew trees, Dartington was re-created in the 1920s by Leonard Elmhirst and his American heiress wife Dorothy as an educational and artistic community. From 1953 it was home to a summer music school founded five years earlier by Sir William Glock, the BBC's head of music, at the suggestion of his teacher the great Arthur Schnabel. Its organising secretary was John Amis, a music critic who had shared a house with Neville in London.

Dartington was the Academy's summer treat, a place for bonding between players. There were parties round the swimming pool for spouses and children, lawn tennis in the afternoons, and table tennis in the evenings. Janet Baker's tennis was almost as competitive as her Bach cantatas and Handel arias, while the violinist Alan Loveday, a fanatical ping-pong player, could be seen trouncing the musicologist Hans Keller. (Though neither, apparently, was a match for the pianist André Tchaikovsky.). Every year a cricket match was played against the Dartington Hall staff, when Neville kept wicket, as he did for the LSO where he still worked. After the game everyone repaired to the White Hart pub at one end of the great house or escaped to the Cott Inn, a twenty-minute walk away through the gardens. The 300 students attended classes, lectures and workshops, and heard a professional concert every evening. It was a chance to meet stellar musicians amd composers such as Britten, Copland, Stravinsky and Peter Maxwell Davies.

The summer school proved a good recruitment ground when four of the original members – Norman Nelson, Simon Streatfeild, John Churchill and Michael Bowie – emigrated (though not as a group) to Canada in the 1960s. [continued on page 72]

Neville Marriner with
George Malcolm.
Photo: Decca

The Dartington Pie Wars

Neville Marriner's love of practical jokes was never better demonstrated than by the tit-for-tat struggle he had with George Malcolm, his brilliant harpsichordist, at Dartington.

In the hope of catching George out in rehearsals, Neville, who marked up all the string parts, would sometimes hand him an unmarked continuo part so that George would find himself playing much too loudly when the strings were playing *pianissimo*, and drowned out when they were playing *forte*.

It was at a concert at Dartington that George decided to take his revenge. The encore one evening was to be a movement from Gluck's *Don Juan*, for strings only, and all playing *pizzicato*. As the strings began, George broke in with a resounding, Gluckian version of 'Over the Hills and Far and Away' which he had composed for himself in advance. John Amis, who was there, described it: 'While they were going *plink-plonk-plink-plonk*, he suddenly let fly with his wonderful invention, a marvellous line, and corpsed the lot of them – the biggest musical come-uppance I've ever seen.'

To pay him back, Neville secretly performed an operation on the chamber organ in the Great Hall that George was due to play on a subsequent evening, taking out the rank of 8-foot pipes. George's grumbling about the weakness of the organ turned to something else when he caught sight of a stack of silver pipes in the corner.

That was not the end of the matter. One night, Neville arrived late and hungry in Dartington, and George offered him a chicken pie, only to discover when he went upstairs to bed that the pie had been returned, half-eaten, to his room. Surreptitiously, he put it back in Neville's room the following morning while Neville was taking a choir rehearsal. But it turned up in his room once more, this time wrapped in his music. The Harries book takes up the story:

'Not to be outdone, George wrapped the pie in a parcel with birthday paper, attached a little note reading "From an admirer in the audience", and had it presented to Neville after that evening's concert, while he was deep in conversation with Sir William Glock. Flattered and unwary, Neville opened it with enthusiasm, and when the pie, now smelly, was revealed in all its glory George knew to expect redress: "I was leaving Dartington early the next morning to go straight to Yehudi Menuhin's festival in Gstaad, and I kept my room locked from that moment onwards. But when I unpacked my bag in the hotel in Gstaad the following day, there inside it was the chicken pie. I still don't know how he did it."'

There was a coda to the story. Many years later, George Malcolm was playing with the Academy chamber ensemble at the Wigmore Hall's 90th anniversary concert. Before he came on, Neville handed a piece of fish to Robert Smissen, the viola player, and told him to put it inside the harpsichord. Bob Smissen said later: 'It was incumbent on me to do it. Malcolm came on stage, and he saw it. He must have had his suspicions…'

[continued from
page 69]
The ping-pong fanatic Alan Loveday was appearing as a soloist at Dartington in 1965 when he was persuaded to join, taking up an invitation he had declined seven years earlier while playing in a trio with Neville and Antony Hopkins. Alan was not just a keen ping-pong player. He was also, in Neville's opinion, the best violinist in England. Record producers thought his tone ideal for Baroque music: pure, intense, and with great projection.

Another new recruit was Carmel Kaine, who was at Dartington in 1967 to play through her programme for the forthcoming International Violin Competition in Vienna. 'She went straight from the back of the Academy's second violins to win the competition.'[12] Anthony Jenkins the viola player was fresh from the Royal Academy of Music when he came in 1970 as one of the extra violas needed for Strauss's *Metamorphosen*. He, too, stayed. Meanwhile a future member was working unrecognised in the Dartington kitchens. Nicholas Kraemer was a music student doing a summer job. He went to every Academy concert, and determined to join one day. He became a regular continuo player in the 1970s.

One of the Academy's greatest stars also arrived at this time, but not from Dartington: the gifted, passionate Iona Brown. Iona had made her solo debut playing the Khachaturian Violin Concerto under Charles Groves, and was to succeed Neville as director of the chamber orchestra eight years later.

Going for the record

Encouraged by Argo, their new recording company, the Academy was moving away from the Baroque and into the late-18th, 19th, and early 20th-century repertoire. During the later 1960s it became primarily a recording orchestra, and leader in the field. By the end of the decade it had 69 records to its name, earning the accolade from H.C. Robbins Landon, the Mozart and Haydn expert of 'finest chamber orchestra in existence.'

But this was after a faltering start. Although well received, the early Argo records did not make a profit, and the contract came close to being cancelled

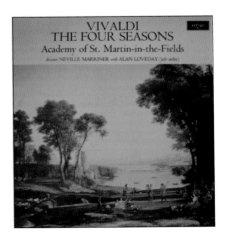

The first best-seller.

after the first year. Once again, the orchestra was saved at the last minute. The very next record, prepared at Dartington in 1967 and recorded that September, was a surprising hit and won an Audio Award. It was of four Rossini string sonatas, rediscovered in the Library of Congress after World War II, and written when the composer was only twelve years old. (Rossini called them 'those horrible sonatas I composed on holiday near Ravenna with my friends… at an early age.'). But they are difficult to bring off technically. A year later, also after a Dartington try-out, came a second lift-off record: Richard Strauss's *Metamorphosen*. But the disc that really established the Academy's name worldwide was Vivaldi's *Four Seasons* with the brilliant Alan Loveday as soloist and Simon Preston on harpsichord and organ. Recorded in St. John's Smith Square in September 1969, it sold enough copies to win a Gold Disc. This was in spite of a difficult recording session. Kingsway Hall was out of use, and St John's had only just been reopened after war-time bomb damage. Its acoustic was unknown, but the resourceful whistling and clapping of the producer, Stan Goodall, satisfied him it would be alright. Then the sound of a pneumatic drill was heard coming from the road outside. At this, the normally peaceable Alan Loveday saw red. He stormed out of the church to confront the workman:

> With his face an inch from the offender's, he enquired belligerently: 'Do you like sex and travel?' To which the unwary drill-operator replied: 'Yes, squire.' Alan's terse, Anglo-Saxon riposte brought howls of approval from the Academy, by now gathered on the steps of the church. And from that moment on, they heard not a single extraneous sound.[13]

Neville went for a highly programmatic version of the *Seasons,* down to the barking of the dog in the 'Spring' movement, supplied by the viola of Stephen Shingles ('They ought to give me a dog licence, I've played the damned dog so often,' he said.) Some critics did not like it, but the public disagreed – the Japanese especially, buying 30,000 copies in the first three months.

Vivaldi, with Mozart, was the composer most congenial to the orchestra's style and the *Four Seasons* – which even in those days was already a staple, receiving some terrible treatment in other hands – became the Academy's signature tune, to such an extent that it made Neville determined to take his orchestra away from the Baroque into a much more varied repertoire, including Dvořák, Grieg, Stravinsky, Bartok, Elgar and Tippett.

John Wilbraham, a regular soloist in the 1960s and 1970s.

Neville's studio magic

Part of the excitement of a concert comes from the visual stimulus of seeing the players while you listen to the music. Argo's engineers were clever at compensating for the lack of this extra emotional impact. They would emphasise a sudden entrance by a section of the orchestra, and highlight a solo. The Argo producer Chris Hazell compared it with putting highlights in hair: 'You're not actually colouring the hair, but emphasising the original colour.'[14]

A great deal was due to Neville's consummate skill as a recording conductor. 'He had a genius for taking a marvellous performance on a recording,' the doyen of London music critics Edward Greenfield told me. 'It was easy enough to do a run-through. That's not the same as having a real performance.' Katherine Adams, the band's road manager, said:

'He was a magician in the studio. Producers thought he had a brilliant ear, and he had a way of calming people down when something was not working. He would talk about something else, then go back. Or if the written notes were marked as a slur, he would have the inside players doing them detached; so what you would hear was an incredibly clear, yet still slurred sound. It wasn't cheating, just a technique.'

Other experiments included close-miking the bass line players and putting Tristan Fry, the timpanist, inside a box of screens and curtains with a microphone so that his drums did not cloud the rest of the sound. John Gray, the double bass, had his own ideas about studio work. By common consent a wonderful player and extraordinarily musical, he irritated Neville with his endless adjustment of stool, instrument and pin. He could not be stopped from re-positioning his own mikes, until one day he picked one up that was not earthed and got a 240-volt reprimand.

Just as everyone thought John Gray was well worth the trouble, so they all recognised that Neville's organising skills were supreme, saving the Academy hours of wasted time in rehearsal and the record companies thousands of pounds in needless studio overtime. Neville aimed for what one violinst called 'clarity, cleanness, and a lack of sentimentality, always a good thing, and especially in Baroque music.'

Neville has always been interested in how things work, and the technical side of recording appealed to him. He was in sympathy with the efforts of the producer and engineer to make a record as lifelike as possible. So he would adopt a slightly faster tempo in the studio, to add excitement, he would shorten crotchets to quavers (with quaver rests) in fast passages, change the instrumentation if necessary, or add extra violins to the top line. He would vary the continuo instrument, using organ, cello or bassoon in place of the harpsichord, and even let into the studio strange creatures like the theorbo and chitarrone, or the violone, an oversized cello that John Gray once brought to work with him.

Acoustics is a peculiar science, and painfully imprecise (although one engineer is said to have declared that a particular studio was bad for the key of E flat). Everything seems to matter, from the paint on the walls to the composition of the furnishings and floorboards. Humidity is absolutely crucial. 'It's like bowling seamers,' Neville says, reaching for the inevitable cricketing metaphor. 'Everything depends on the weather.'

In London the greatest danger was ambient noise. In the summer of 1971, Iona Brown was recording for Argo one of her favourite pieces, *The Lark Ascending* by Vaughan Williams, at the Kingsway Hall. The hall was liked by Argo because it made a chamber orchestra sound like a symphony orchestra. Unfortunately, it had the London Underground running beneath it. On this occasion Mike Bremner, the producer, and Stan Goodall, the engineer, were in the control box listening to Iona play what they decided was the perfect 'take'. But as her final, beautiful note faded into wonderstruck silence, a Tube train rumbled past below them.

> Hearing it through the headphones, Stan turned to Mike, his face contorted in agony: 'Just the wind in the trees, Stan,' muttered Mike. And that is how the record ends, with the lark ascending to the faint rustle of wind-blown leaves on the Piccadilly Line.[15]

In other cases, the problems were more psychological. Quite frequently, nothing at all would go right. It happened with the recording of *Eine Kleine Nachtmusik*, when the sound was feeble for hours, and nothing usable emerged. But after the break, the players came back and did the whole thing in one take. Another trick, if the players failed to produce the wanted sound, was to let them play right through, wrong notes and all, then pretend that only a fault in the equipment required them to do it again. Neville had his own tricks to save time: when a sudden change of tempo was required, for instance, he might get the band to play across the double bar in the old tempo, go back and play again in the new tempo, then cut and stitch the two takes together. 'A bit naughty,' said one player. 'But why not?'

Because of his intensive preparation of scores, Neville was able to record in long takes – perhaps the most spectacular being his *Metamorphosen*, which reportedly was done with only one splice. But if many repeats were required, he had the temperament to maintain a concert atmosphere, countering the players' *ennui* with jokes. He found humorous ways of correcting individuals: 'I think we're all sharp except for that fiddle at the back,' he would say.[16]

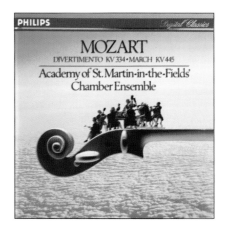

In the early days of the democratic collective it was common for a lot of players to crowd into the control room to listen to the takes and discuss the finer points of interpretation. But as with concert rehearsals, so much discussion came to be seen as a luxury, and Neville's word was increasingly decisive. As an example of his ruthless efficiency, we can jump ahead a couple of years to the Academy's recording for Philips of thirty of the Mozart symphonies (and one by his father Leopold). Before this the orchestra had played only four or five of these. But the series took only 41 sessions to put on vinyl (a session is half a day), over a period of 11 months. The secret was that Neville was able to mark up the parts for the band in their absence, since by now the players knew his style so well.

First steps into Europe

The records were being pumped out at an ever increasing rate, but the players themselves were rarely visible in their own country. A series of five concerts on the South Bank during the 1968-9 season, one of them featuring The King's Singers in their London debut, helped put faces to names.

Continental audiences got a chance to look, too. One of the first trips was to the Flanders Festival in Bruges, in 1967 at the invitation of Franz Vanagt, who owned a record shop in the city. This led to a two-week tour through France (*le tour gastronomique*, as it became known, since the food was infinitely better than the hotels) with the pianist Philippe Entremont.

But the key tour was to Holland, organised by executives of Phonogram, Decca's distributor in Holland, whose interest had been sparked not only by the

Academy's sound but by its informal manner and democratic constitution. To their ears, the band's cumbersome name sounded attractively English. A hat-trick of three successive Edison Awards, the music prize given by Dutch record producers and distributors, followed in 1968, 1969 and 1970. The band was invited over to play at the Edison gala concert in Amsterdam's Concertgebouw, and secured its first tour of Germany, the beginning of a long and productive relationship with the agent Hans Ulrich Schmid, one of the most important in the orchestra's life. At first Herr Schmid was not too happy about the new client's name, and changed it to 'London Strings' – a marketing decision which he later regretted. As he conceded: 'At that time I did not dare to present them under their proper name, which seemed to be too long, and I had the feeling nobody would have any idea what it really means! How time has changed!...Today I must say I am ashamed because this name ['London Strings'] was not too full of fantasy.'[17] Germany was to become, with the U.S., the band's most important touring market.

In the same year, 1967, a smaller ensemble of eight players – the front desks minus the bass – was created in order to play the Mendelssohn Octet for the radio. The BBC wanted the piece done by a cohesive group, not – as often happens – by two string quartets in competition. The following year the group recorded it for Argo, with Hugh Maguire leading and Neville beside him. Then known simply as 'The Octet', its official title was 'The Academy of St Martin in the Fields Chamber Ensemble'. The numbers engaged ranged from eight down to three; wind and brass players would be involved as the music required.

As the repertoire expanded and the workload increased, so did the number of players that the Academy kept on its books. The increasing need for wind players meant the number of strings had to be increased for balance. The Academy was now fielding three kinds of orchestra (though not of course at the same time): a chamber band of 16 or 20 players; an ensemble of eight or fewer; and a classical symphony orchestra of 40 plus. In 1973, a fourth element appeared when the Academy Chorus was formed.[18]

It became clear that adminstratively and financially, things would have to be formalized. In 1970 it was decided that the Academy must become a limited company. The 'Academy of St Martin in the Fields Orchestra Ltd.' created in 1971 had the five section principals as directors: Neville Marriner, Trevor Connah, Stephen Shingles, Kenneth Heath and John Gray. (Macolm Latchem joined the Board shortly afterwards.) It was well understood who was Number One, however.

Not a few people were unhappy with the move. Liz Williams, who a year or two before had joined as assistant manager, remembers trudging round the marshes outside Aldeburgh that Christmas with Molly while the band was recording in the Maltings, when Molly said: 'I don't think the Academy will ever be the same again.'

The Academy at Leixslip Castle, Co. Kildare, home of the Hon. Desmond Guinness. Shown in picture, L to R: Timothy Brown, Iona Brown , Andrew McGee, Malcolm Latchem, Roy Gillard, Alan Cuckston, Stephen Shingles, Anthony Jenkins, Denis Vigay, Roger Smith. Raymund Koster .

Painting by Philippa Garner

Chapter Four

NEVILLE STANDS UP

THE new constitution was a sign of the Academy's maturity, and a signal of its leader's intent. As Molly Marriner had predicted, things would not be the same again.

But she was only half right. Certainly, the small family enterprise run from the Marrriner flat off Gloucester Road was disappearing, to be replaced by an institution with a growing international reputation. But the relationship between Neville and the band, though altered, remained as strong as ever.

Neville himself needed little encouragement from record companies to leave the Baroque behind and lead the orchestra into new repertoire, first into the classical age of J C Bach, Haydn, and Mozart and, beginning with Beethoven, into the more manageable compositions of the Romantic era. In any case, the Academy's sparsely-populated niche was being invaded by others: chamber groups were sprouting to copy the 'authentic' style and the Baroque composers with whom the early Academy had made its mark were being commandeered by 'period' instrument bands – one of which was set up by Christopher Hogwood, a former Academy continuo player.[1]

The pressure of recording compelled Neville to compromise the democratic principles of the early Academy. He abandoned his own prejudices about conductors not only because he was compelled to, but because by now he had decided to become one himself.

In fulfilling his own ambition to become a conductor, he may have thought he was making space for the Academy to find its own way in the world. But his determination that the Academy should have the best possible chance of survival in a competitive market meant that he could not stand back – and nor, by all accounts, were the players keen that he should.

The 1970s and 1980s, two decades of growth and fame – and the troubles they brought with them – will be reviewed in the next chapter. In this, we shall focus on the relationship between Neville Marriner and his orchestra. That relationship is the *basso continuo* of the Academy story, and Neville's decision to pursue a seperate career also marked a watershed in the Academy's fortunes. Neville took a step back, yet remained the dominant influence. As far as the audiences were concerned, nothing had changed. If anything, the association became stronger in the public's mind. The step he took might have resulted eventually in a clean break, but it did not. Why it did not, we shall try to explain by sketching his career and his character.

Neville in America

The opportunity came out of a blue sky. It was a letter from Joseph Troy, a Californian attorney, inviting Neville to become the conductor of a chamber orchestra which he was founding with two friends in Los Angeles to provide an artistic outlet for Hollywood studio and recording musicians. His partners were both keen amateur musicians: James Arkatov, a life insurance salesman who played the cello, was artistic director, and Richard Colburn, an industrialist and viola player, was putting up the money.

Though the Academy was not yet well known in America, Troy knew about Neville from his Argo releases, and convinced the partners to bid for him. Outside the recording studio, Neville had very little experience as a conductor. He had done a few engagements in England with the LSO, some work with the Cambridge University Music Society for David Willcocks, and with the BBC Symphony Orchestra. But the Americans may not have realised that, misled (as Neville says) by his title of 'director' at the Academy: in America 'director' or 'musical director' usually means chief conductor. No doubt Neville was careful

Richard Colburn, the
musical philanthropist, with
the young Leila Josefowicz
and Robert Lipseth.
Photo: Paul Siemion

not to disabuse them. Whether it took a series of letters to persuade him, or just one telephone call (memories differ on this), in 1969, he and Molly were on the plane to Los Angeles. Neville left his violin behind, deliberately.

The couple had been told they would be housed, but had no idea what to expect. It was a Saturday when they took off and Molly, ever practical, realising that the shops would have shut for the weekend when they arrived, told Neville to save as much salt, pepper and butter as he could from the airplane, just in case. Neville continues the story:

'We were met at the airport by a stretch limousine and driven through the Californian evening to this house in Beverley Hills, with an entrance like this…[he threw his arms wide]… the biggest swimming pool I have ever seen, pale blue, and the sound of Heifetz playing the 'Scottish Fantasy', very softly throughout. The house was glass – and it was all ours, along with three servants and six cars. We never looked back.'

This was the Colburn compound; and here for three months a year for the next decade it was home. Among the neighbours were the singer Eartha Kitt, and the 'strange' record producer Phil Spector who liked to wave pistols around (and was jailed years later for shooting a girl friend). One day Darryl Zanuck's pet monkey escaped and they watched it being chased across the lawns by a little girl, the butler, and assorted gardeners. Another neighbour, as it happened, was Jascha Heifetz. And when after the couple had settled in and Neville was asked by a newspaper whom he would most like to meet in Hollywood, he had no hesitation in nominating Heifetz, whom, he revered, and the actress Goldie

Hawn because he had seen her in the TV series *Rowan and Martin's Laugh-in*. 'And, dammit, they both turned up at the first concert,' he told me. 'Goldie's dad had been a violin player, and she paid for her own ticket.' Heifetz he remembers meeting first at a party at Dick Colburn's house, when the violinist arrived with a wonderful blonde on his arm: 'I asked him how I should introduce the lady. "I don't know", said Heifetz in his thick accent. "I only rented her." He had reached the absolute peak of perfection as a player, but he was incapable of keeping friends, and very lonely.' Neville later played Heifetz at table tennis – he lost – and once borrowed a violin to play chamber music with him. For ever after he liked to tell interviewers that that was what finally decided him to give up the violin. It was a good note to end on.

Later the Colburn compound would become the temporary home of the soloists that came to perform with the Los Angeles Chamber Orchestra: including Alfred Brendel, Gervase de Peyer and Barry Tuckwell.

Life in Los Angeles was certainly colourful, but not always easy for Molly – not least because, although she had six cars at her disposal, she was unable to drive. Her husband seemed to thrive on it, taking to the high life enthusiastically and enjoying the celebrity status that was conferred on him. Dick Colburn was ever attentive. Molly remembers him ringing one day from Australia to ask 'What are you doing on Saturday? Nothing? Well, keep it free!' And he flew back to LA to play in a string quartet with Neville, returning to Australia the following day.

Neville's first job was to begin weeding out , as tactfully as he could, some of the players who had been chosen before his arrival. They included buddies of the founders, or people who had sent cases of whisky to lubricate the selection process. Jim Arkatov had been appointed principal cellist, which was a surprise in

Neville Marrriner with Barry Tuckwell, an Academy regular in the 1960s.

Photo: Reg Wilson

what was meant to be a professional outfit. But in his account of things, Neville says only how 'wonderful' the players were: 'The fiddlers were all pupils of Heifetz and the cellists of Piatigorsky. They played in the Continental [that is European] style; and they could play anything. The wind players were from the studios, the best in the world.' He ruffled some feathers back home by telling one interviewer that the Americans were technically more gifted than British players, although much less receptive musically, especially when it came to ensemble work.

Unfortunately, the founding triumvirate of LACO were not always of the same mind. Dick Colburn wanted a band that played baroque and Mozart, music not covered by the Los Angeles Symphony. According to his daughter Carol, he was unhappy when the repertoire moved away. After Neville left the orchestra, Colburn and Troy had a falling-out, and Colburn detached himself but remained a generous supporter of Neville's enterprises.

LACO was Neville's first serious conducting job, but it was not the first time he had conducted. He had been thinking about making the jump for some years. In 1963, when he was just 40, he had taken lessons at Pierre Monteux's summer school for conductors at Hancock, in Maine. Monteux, then with the LSO, had seen him directing the Academy in rehearsal, and urged him to 'stand up and conduct like a man.' Also invited was his friend Erik Smith, the musically gifted son of the German conductor Hans Schmidt-Isserstedt who was at that time a young producer with Decca and destined to become the pilot of the Academy's drive into the symphonic repertoire. Looking back years later on that summer, Erik said: 'At least one of us came back a conductor.'[2] Monteux's style was collaborative rather than confrontational, which chimed in with Neville's role at the Academy. He stressed the importance of doing as much as possible in rehearsal. When it came to the concert, he did little more than remind the players – and that with his eyes. His gestures were contained within a small frame, his hands rarely going above his head, an example Neville followed:

Erik Smith in retirement reading his favourite composer.

Photo: Hans Skarrup

'I'd already observed the kind of conductors Monteux hated – the "choreogra-phobantic" conductors with big gestures who levitate. He always said they were entertaining the audience rather than helping the orchestra. The other day I saw [Gustavo] Dudamel in LA. He's fantastic and levitates *all* the time. On the other hand, it's enormously effective. He gets the attention of the orchestra all the time. I didn't mind, because the result was so good. Some think they can stimulate an orchestra with physical gestures. But most of the players will have decided how they are going to respond to a conductor, and if they don't like what he is doing, it won't make any difference.'

This seems to be a general rule. Liz Marriner, the wife of Neville's clarinet-tist son Andrew, is a psychotherapist who has studied the the rapport – or lack of it – between players and conductors. She told me that conductors who can communicate by a gesture or hint are popular; those who talk about the music, however eloquently, are often disliked.

In his youth Neville had played under Toscanini, Szell, Furtwängler, Cantelli and Karajan. Musically, the conductor who originally inspired him was the Viennese Josef Krips, who was principal conductor of the LSO before Neville joined and showed how an orchestra could be persuaded to play classical music in a more sophisticated way. 'People used to play Beethoven symphonies because they knew them almost with their eyes shut. Joe insisted "open your eyes, and look at me, too."'

For discipline, the model was George Szell: 'He was the last of the sonofa-bitch conductors. He and Stokowski.' By discipline, Neville means two things. First, attention to detail in preparation of the score. He used to raid the library in Cleveland, the home of Szell's symphony orchestra, for the conductor's scores in order to examine his marks and see how he would re-edit Schumann and Dvořák symphonies where he thought the orchestration weak. For him, as for Szell, 95 percent of what the audience hears in a concert has been prepared. 'You're lucky if you have an orchestra with soloists [principals] who add something of their own. Not many give you that freedom.'

The intensity of his preparation, as detailed for concerts as for recordings, and the contrast with the modesty of his gestures, is Neville Marriner's defining feature as a conductor.

The other kind of discipline he learned from Szell, was his intolerance – not of players, but of inferior playing. Until the law changed in the late 1950s, American conductors were more or less free to hire and fire. Orchestras had

30-week seasons, and a conductor could tell a player not to bother coming back. But when 52-week contracts were introduced to give players security, that power evaporated. Szell managed to keep his players up to the mark even so, Neville said. 'I admired him for that.' From the outset, Neville insisted that the Academy be a freelance outfit; and to this day there are no contracts. 'What I wanted was the ability to be able to say "Don't come back, please, because you're not really what we want." We didn't want people suing for wrongful dismissal.' Neville has never lost his dislike for contracts and unions, which he regards as musical feather-bedding. He remains convinced that salaried players will inevitably become lazy and bored; and in Britain, at least, many players agree with him.

The first time Neville actually stood up to conduct was shortly after his time with Monteux when, at another summer school, he directed the Dartington chorus. But the occasion which has passed into the mythology was in November, 1967, when the Academy was recording Stravinsky's *Apollo* and *Pulcinella* ballet suites at the Kingsway Hall in London. After a series of ragged starts, so the story goes, with Neville vainly gesturing with his bow from the leader's desk, the oboist Roger Lord piped up: 'Nev – if you're going to conduct, would you mind standing somewhere where we can see you… or somewhere where we can't.'[3] Edward Greenfield was at the rehearsal. 'I remember him directing with violin in hand, waving his bow. It was a great moment. Marvellous. And it is one of my favourite discs.'

In 1969, Neville had given up his day job at the LSO. He was 45. But although did not take his violin to America, he continued to play it on concert tours with the Academy. Like much else in his career, the change was gradual. Neville cannot remember the last time he led the Academy playing his violin. It seems to have been at a concert in Wuppertal, Germany, in 1975.

While working with the Los Angeles Chamber Orchestra, Neville was also appointed associate conductor of the Northern Sinfonia in Newcastle upon Tyne from 1971 to 1973, with whom he made several records. From 1975-7 he succeeded André Previn as adviser to the Greater London Council for the South Bank Summer Music concerts at the Queen Elizabeth Hall. During the LACO contract, and helped by his new agent, Stephen Wright, he secured invitations from a number of American symphony orchestras to conduct Bach, Haydn or Mozart in festivals or for weekend concerts when their own conductors were taking a break: the Boston Symphony at Tanglewood, the Chicago at Ravinia, the Philadelphia at Blossom. He performed at the Lincoln Center, in Kansas City, Milwaukee and Buffalo, where Michael Tilson Thomas let him choose his own programmes.

By degrees he was able, as a *quid pro quo* to smuggle some Schumann, Brahms or Tchaikovsky into his guest appearances, or ask for engagements during the main winter season. But the big break came the following year, when he got his own symphony orchestra – the Minnesota Orchestra in Minneapolis, one of five that had expressed an interest in him.

A symphony of his own

He took up the post in September, 1979, on a contract requiring four months a year. The first encounter with a unionized, salaried, highly-paid American symphony orchestra came as a shock. After two weeks' rehearsal for his first concert with the new band, the players warned they might go on strike. Although he didn't know it, this was a standard gambit when a new music director arrived, a chance to get a pay rise.

> 'My manager advised me to go home. "Anything you do will be wrong," he said. So I got on an aeroplane and went back to London. I'd been back in the house barely an hour when the phone rang to say the strike was over. Of course, it was a damp squib. I'd never worked with orchestras that went on strike. It left a bad taste in my mouth.'

Although never a poor timekeeper, he was appalled to discover that the union insisted on a clock being visible on stage during rehearsal. On one occasion, when he was 50 bars from the end of a piece, a hand shot up to warn him that he was into overtime. Concerts were deemed to be over when the conductor lowered his baton, which made encores difficult.

Neville found it hard to accept the idea of players sitting on the management Board of an orchestra – though he came himself from a player-controlled band, the LSO, and since 1970 had had player directors on the Board of his own Academy. At Minneapolis he never got on with them; his view of them as better politicians than musicians probably did not escape their attention. His dislike of the new unionized regime seems to have been shared by many younger players. In an article about Neville's time at Minneapolis, a leading American music writer noted a paradox: that when conductors were free to behave like tyrants, jobs in symphony orchestras were highly prized. But when players got job security and salaries, older musicians became cynical and younger ones preferred to play in chamber orchestras. Neville's comment was: 'There should be an element of insecurity in all artists' lives, just to keep them sharp.'

Neville Marriner conducting the Minnesota Orchestra on a return visit in 2003.
Photo: Star Tribune

Union restrictions and high salaries made recording difficult in America which is why London became the recording Mecca in that golden age. With LACO he made only four records, and with the Minnesota Orchestra only six. But he did tour the U.S. with them, and went to Australia. Rehearsing on tour was also forbidden, apparently, but Neville managed to get the players to agree to half-hour sessions in 'important cities', enough at least to test the acoustics of halls in advance.

He tried rehearsing the Minnesota as if it was a chamber orchestra, but quickly learned that that was too expensive: the strings could not be rehearsed separately without paying the whole orchestra. And there was no time – or at least time was too expensive – to have discussions with the players. Neville aimed to follow the lead of Herbert von Karajan, getting as much detail done as he could without boring the players to tears.

If Neville was disappointed in retrospect with aspects of his job in the Twin Cities of Minneapolis and St. Paul – he felt he never succeeded in getting them to play Mozart quite in the way he wanted – they also did, he said, 'very good things.' He was impressed by the extraordinary support for the orchestra in the community, something he had never seen in Europe. Rich subscribers heading south to escape the bitter winters would send their tickets back to the office so that they could be sold again, with the result that for five or six years the auditorium was selling more than a 100 per cent of its seats. Audiences discovered a new sound to compare with that of former directors Ormandy, Mitropoulos, Dorati and Neville's immediate predecessor Stanislav Skrowaczewski. They saw what one critic described as 'a trim and sporty Englishman' looking much younger than his age with 'a touch of gray in his blond hair and quite handsome in a professorial way.' (Though he was never blond and 'professorial' is an odd word to choose).

During this time, while working with the Cleveland Orchestra, Neville got a message from Glenn Gould. The brilliant eccentric wanted to record with him all the Beethoven piano concertos before he reached the age of 50. They met for a late-afternoon breakfast in Toronto where Gould lived, and talked until lunch – at midnight – when Gould declared that he liked to record a minute of music per hour, and suggested playing the solo parts and sending them to London where the Academy could wrap the accompaniment around them. 'We agreed,' said Neville. 'And then he died.' Gould must have had a presentiment: he was just 50 when he died, in October 1982.

Minneapolis was the setting for a rare but wonderful Marriner gaffe which Neville loves telling against himself. The occasion, broadcast live on state-wide TV in September, 1982 was a special Scandinavian musical gala – Minneapolis is home to a large population of Scandinavian immigrants – attended by royal personages from Denmark, Sweden and Norway. Victor Borge, the Danish-American comedian, as well as playing his musical jokes on the piano, had been due to introduce the distinguished soloists, who included Judith Blegen, Hakan Hagegard, Martti Talvela, and the Swedish dramatic soprano Birgit Nilsson. At the last minute, Borge said he couldn't do the introductions due to a sore throat. The Minnesota management begged Neville to take the job on: 'It's you or nobody,' they said. Reluctantly, Neville agreed. Things went well until Birgit Nilsson came out, resplendent in a sparkling black dress, her black hair showing no trace of grey (though she was 64 years old) with medal ribbons on her chest and a gold medallion hanging down her front. After she had sung her first number, an aria from Wagner or Strauss, Neville turned to begin their broadcast chat. He

[continued on page 92]

The Modest Maestro

The first thing you notice about Sir Neville Marriner is his complete lack of self-importance. The people he meets on tour call him 'maestro' because that is the convention, but there is nothing of the maestro in his manner. What you see is an affable, easy-going man with a mischievous sense of humour, looking much younger than his years.

No doubt Sir Neville enjoys the perks of maestrodom: the shining black limo that conveys him from concert hall to hotel, the respectful bow of the fur-mantled commissionaire who greets him on the hotel steps, the grin of the uniformed lad who shows him to his room. He likes the fact that the Hotel Imperial in Vienna displays his photograph in the lobby when he is staying there (Herbert von Karajan enjoyed the same honour), and that (like Karajan) he is given the key to the back door that opens directly onto the narrow street separating the hotel from the Musikverein.

But Neville has the common touch, and treats everyone alike. He has a persuasive charm that puts ordinary folk at ease, attracts patrons and donors and inspires great affection, even love, in his players. When he hears himself praised, he re-directs the compliment immediately towards somebody else. He is critical of his own skill as a violinist and of his ability as a conductor.

His sense of humour is his most obvious characteristic – and his greatest weapon. 'He uses his humour and razor wit to make his point,' says Christopher Cowie, principal oboist and one of the players on the Board. 'It's not like talking to an 85-year-old. He pretends to be bemused in order to draw you out, but he's operating at a higher speed than you are.' As a young man Neville Marriner showed no fear of personages: he was cheeky with conductors and familiar with musical bigwigs. He loved practical jokes, like putting grasshoppers into people's violins. He fondly recalls his youthful exploits, for example the day he went up in a Tiger Moth with his friend Peter Gibbs, a former RAF pilot, and bombed the LSO tour bus with flour bags on the road from Brussels to Ostend. He is able to take a joke against himself, too, as on the occasion when four of his players attempted to give him a ducking for making critical remarks about the Chorus at an end-of-tour dinner.

Neville's natural intelligence gives him a great command of words as well as of music. His colourful rebukes have become famous: conducting the Bayerische Rundfunk orchestra, for example, he complained that the *pizzicato* in the basses had no resonance, sounding 'like a golf ball hitting a dead sheep.' He made life easy for magazine and newspaper interviewers with his fluency and candour.

Usually he chooses his words carefully, to indicate his feelings without giving offence. But Neville's humour can be sardonic, even biting when he is upset: Iona Brown once described it as 'lethal'. 'He could be really mean sometimes, especially to wind players,' a fond supporter said. 'He has mellowed, but can still be sharp if things are not right, or he feels insecure. I did enjoy his humour,' said another. Some of the younger players are sorry to have missed the barbs of his earlier years.

As his friend and colleague Erik Smith neatly put it: 'Making music is a serious – not an earnest – businesss, and humour helps to accomplish it.' Erik described Neville as 'mercurial', quick to see both sides of a question and to grasp a musical or technical problem. He was always ready with solutions, 'always the sharpest tool in the box', in the words of one writer.

Slow to give praise (a habit he may have learned from his own father), Neville is exceptionally generous with money. He made a very large loan from his own bank account to a player who wanted to buy a fiddle, and always foots the bill when family and friends are gathered. Once, on tour, he famously told the band that the last-night party was on him, and to put all the drinks on his bill. The account that was presented next morning was enormous. Neville signed it without demur, only remarking that 'it must have been a good party.' Some time later, an embarrassed hotel manager rang up to apologize: Neville had been charged not only for the drinks, but for all the hotel rooms as well.

After his humour, it is the man's energy that stands out. The Academy's 50th anniversary year saw its founding director turn 85. Yet he was still playing tennis and conducting orchestras all over Europe and beyond.

His stamina was illustrated in 2008 when Murray Perahia had to drop out of the Academy's U.S. tour at the last minute because of an infected hand. The American promoters warned that unless Neville stepped in the tour would collapse. Neville cancelled a forthcoming engagement at Zagreb to take Murray Perahia's place as conductor, flying over the Easter weekend from Ruse in Bulgaria to Houston, Texas, with only a few hours stop-over to collect clothes in London.

Behind the humour, the charm, and the apparent effortlessness hides a determined man. When it comes to music and its performance, Neville can be quite ruthless, a perfectionist who is liable to take for granted the efforts and achievements of his players. Although sensitive to criticism and slights, he very rarely shows anger. Only an icy manner betrays it. Occasions on which he lost his temper are hard to find: it did happen once, many years ago, at a concert in Germany when the double bass John Gray was plainly leading the bass section from the back in

Learning Britten's
War Requiem at
home in 2009.
Photo: Christian Tyler

competition with Neville on the front desk. After the concert, according to one witness, he chased the bass player round the backstage corridors 'shouting like mad'.

Marriner has shown himself to be a natural leader: the boss who is not bossy, and charms people into doing what he wants. As we have seen, he prefers benign autocracy to messy democracy – at least when it comes to orchestras. But he is no podium bully. His wife Molly recalls with pride a music critic at the Salzburg Festival remarking that when Herbert von Karajan conducted his protégée the violinist Anne-Sophie Mutter, he was like a fierce father. When Neville conducted her, he was more like 'a loving grandfather'. ('Though whether Neville liked being called a "grandfather,"' adds Molly, 'I'm not sure!').

His managerial ability was noted many years ago by Trevor Connah, one of the original directors of the 1971 company:

'I don't think the Academy would have survived it [becoming a limited company] if it hadn't been for Neville's organising powers, and the terrific standard of the playing. The music wouldn't have been enough to keep them together, and the thing would have collapsed. People would have left.'

A good head for business and an instinct for market opportunities are other facets of this versatile musician. Those like the critic Edward Greenfield who have observed him over the decades see an ambitious musical entrepreneur, a man who caught the tide, creating three orchestras, hiring the right players, choosing the right repertoire, chasing up the record companies, and seizing the chances offered first by stereo LPs, and then by CDs.

Minutes of Board meetings show a decisive director with a good grasp of figures, who found practical solutions when things got tough. Directors and players alike tended to rely implicitly on his judgement, and found it difficult later to adjust to his absence. Outsiders noticed this business acumen, too. He was once invited to a high-level businessman's conference in Switzerland. Seeing a good opportunity to button-hole tycoons for sponsorship, Neville accepted gladly. He was disconcerted to discover on arrival that the organisers wanted him to give a talk on 'Leadership'.

Many younger musicians have profited from his influence. He spotted the talent of the Canadian violinist Leila Josefowicz when she was hardly into her teens, and gave her a concert debut with the Academy. After hearing the young Russian conductor Vasily Petrenko at a competition in Spain, he helped him win the job of principal conductor at the Royal Liverpool Philharmonic in 2006. Neville rarely goes to concerts for pleasure – he finds himself always acting the critic – and avoids piano recitals because, he says, the solo piano has little 'colour'.

The Marriners have a range of friends that extends well outside music: actors and theatre directors, painters, writers and broadcasters. One of their oldest friends is Sir David Attenborough, who served for many years on the Academy Board.

The couple collect paintings and ceramics, while Neville has a particular enthusiasm for antique clocks, for puzzles and gadgets of all kinds, and for designing improvements to the family's country house.

The three grandchildren – three boys – have inherited some musical ability; Douglas, the child of Andrew Marriner the clarinettist and his wife Liz, has become an accomplished jazz drummer, founding his own quintet at the Trinity College of Music in London.

One of the Marriner family institutions is the annual cricket match which they host at Chardstock in Devon, pitting Academy players against the village team on a steeply-sloping pitch with a wonderful view. The three grandsons have inherited some of their grandfather's sporting prowess, as well as his musical ability.

At the beach with the grandsons –
L to R. Douglas, Milo and Matthew.

[continued from
page 89] asked her about the medallion. 'Ah, this was given to me by His Majesty himself!' she said, looking up at the royal box. 'And what about these two big ones here?' Neville continued, his hands gesturing towards the diva's majestic bosom. There was an awful silence, while the *double entendre* sank in. The expression froze on Neville's face, while the diva looked stumped. Behind them, the orchestral players were cracking up. An interminable few seconds passed while Neville recovered, and continued: 'This one is rather special, isn't it?' he said, his hand moving quickly away from the danger zone. Birgit ralllied like the pro she was, joking that this medal entitled her to be called 'Commander', which, she said, had rather vexed her husband.

Neville, a naturally fluent talker, never again addressed a big audience without a script in his pocket.

During his time at Minneapolis, Neville had a holiday job as music director of the Meadow Brook Festival, the summer season of the Detroit Symphony. This was a mixed blessing. Although an excellent place for music out of doors without the need for amplification, it meant very little time off for reading or tennis. Other jobs he had running in parallel were principal guest conductor of the Berlin Radio Symphony, of the Orchestre National de France, and chief conductor of the Stuttgart Radio Orchestra [*Südwestfunk-Orchester*], a job which took up about three months a year but which allowed him greater freedom of repertoire, and much more recording than was possible in the U.S. His predecessor at Stuttgart was Sergiu Celibidache, a major figure who was used to getting eight or ten rehearsals for each concert but has no interest in recording. 'Celibidache was a great talker, and for the first two or three he would talk,' Neville says. 'And as I wasn't particularly articulate in German anyway, we were able to convert many of those rehearsals into recording sessions.'

In 1986 the Minnesota contract ended: he had done eight years, involving a hundred different programmes every three years: a hard thing to do, he said, in front of people who have played the pieces more often than you have conducted them. Now London became Neville's base again, and the expanded Academy orchestra (the 'big band') his prime concern.

A year after taking up the Minneapolis job, Neville was awarded the CBE; as he left it, he received a knighthood. For some of his old friends 'Sir Neville' was a little difficult to get used to. One who adapted quickly was Ian Bonner ('Bonzo'), the loyal truck driver, who had been calling him 'Nev' for years. He couldn't go on doing that, he felt, but 'Sir Neville' sounded downright unfriendly. He found the compromise: from now on, it was 'Snev'.

Marriner was not to have an outside orchestra again, but for the next 20 years he received invitations to conduct bands of all kinds in many countries. He formed a particular attachment with the Cadaques Chamber Orchestra which he conducts each Spring at their festival at the Peralada castle in north-east Spain. He has made a number of recordings with them.

These days the Academy is making only a couple of records a year. But Neville's own schedule hardly seems to flag. When he is not taking the Academy 'big band' on tour (he takes them down the Rhine every New Year) or for its rarer concerts in London, he is off round the world. In 2009, his own 85th anniversary, he has been to Germany four more times, to Vienna twice, and to Sofia, Zagreb, Dublin and Melbourne. In September, he accepted a remarkable challenge: to conduct Britten's *War Requiem* in Gdansk, Poland, in honour of those killed in the Nazi blitzkrieg invasion of Poland 70 years before. A challenge, because it is a work he has never conducted – although he played in the first performance and first recording of it as principal second violin in the LSO.[4] His schedule for 2010 includes the U.S., Romania, Lausanne, Strasbourg, Berne, Berlin and Tokyo.

The record partnership

Once described as 'the most prominent phonographic musician of our time,' Sir Neville has made, with the Academy, more records than any other pairing of director-conductor and orchestra. His overall total, of about 600 discs, has been surpassed only by Karajan (whose score contains many re-recording). That means something like 1,500 pieces of music which he has pored over, edited and marked up for recording in more than half a century.[5]

But the biggest step in music, the single step onto the conductor's podium, was not without its tribulations, even for a man of Neville's confidence, charm and thoroughness. Raymond Keenlyside, interviewed in 1980, said 'Neville was for ages a dreadful conductor. In the early days we didn't need to be brought in at such-and-such a bar.' Interviewed by John Amis for BBC Television's 'Music Now' programme in 1970, Neville said it had been difficult to convince the outside world that a violinist, the leader of a chamber orchestra, could conduct a symphony orchestra. 'But', he added, 'violinists are much closer to the repertoire than conductors who come to it through piano playing.'

As we have seen, the 'democratic centralism' of the chamber music days was not really sustainable in a symphony orchestra. Leading the string band was a matter of control by consent: it did not require anyone to beat time or point up all the entries, only be mindful of sound quality, articulation, fingerings and dynamics. Now the regime was centralism without the democracy, reinforced by Neville's almost ruthless determination to get things right, but softened by his capacity for diplomacy and charm, and that characteristic ability to defuse tension with humour. 'I wouldn't call it diplomacy, really,' Neville told an interviewer in 1986, 'but more a question of how much you can press a player to change before you meet with complete resistance..You must be able to give way yourself.' If things were not coming together at all, he added, the trick was to begin with the most inflexible players and try to get the flexible ones to work around them.

At the podium he has a number of tricks. For example, he does not look directly at a player about to make an important entry – it only adds to the pressure they are already under. Instead, he will look at some invisible person beyond them. If they do something really badly, he looks down 'and this means you have been spanked,' according one player.[6]

In his search for perfection, others told me, Neville picks almost randomly on players to keep them up to the mark. His way of recognising a perfect piece of playing is to give a wry smile and look away. When he considers a performance perfect, he complains. Why? To make sure it's perfect again next time. Because he is slow to thank the players for what they have achieved, recalls principal oboist Christopher Cowie, when he does so, they never forget it. In a speech at the British Council in Berlin in 2007 Neville said it was having the best players which had carried him through. 'It was a very moving moment. I took a photo.'

A less obvious difficulty was nerves. Neville's approach to conducting was for ever governed by his memory of life as a fiddle player; and standing in front of his own colleagues he was never quite as confident as he appeared, or as he felt with other orchestras. At first sight that seems surprising: after all, he knows the Academy better than any musicians in the world. The reason, of course, is that they know *him* better than anyone else. He never forgets that his friends behind the desks remain as free-spirited – even mutinous at times – as he had been himself.

This feeling of insecurity is something he rarely admits to – and practically never to his players – but is familiar to other musicians brave (or rash) enough to stand up in front of orchestras of which they were once members. Neville felt it when conducting his old orchestra, the LSO, just as Haitink did when with the

Concertgebouw, where he was a second violin, and Giulini, a former viola player with La Scala.

Players recall that he could at times become very cross in recording sessions. He was noticeably scratchy during the recordings of the Mozart piano concertos he made with Alfred Brendel. This may have been, according to one who knew him well, because he was a little in awe of Brendel's musicianship. ('Brendel was very nice about it, so everything went fine.') The same thing would happen when he was conducting at Salzburg, Karajan's birthplace and stamping ground, where he felt the status-conscious maestro was hovering in the wings: on at least one occasion Karajan sent his secretary over to watch the Academy at work.

Even after ten years on the podium, Neville was still able to say: 'In other orchestras, particularly symphony orchestras, players rarely pass comment. When you're conducting your friends, at the very least your close acquaintances, they'll all tell you if they don't like something, and somewhat pungently, too. They still make me work for my podium.'[7] And in 2009, at dinner after a particularly rousing concert with the big band at the Musikverein in Vienna, Neville joked: 'They'll just about put up with me, but in the end they'd rather have no conductor at all.'

Maybe so. Yet they still feel it is something of a special event when he is there to conduct them. Chris Cowie said: 'He makes a big difference. He's very businesslike, and he appears not to do much, but has this way of making a difference.' Even when he is not present in the flesh, some feel his spirit hovering over them. 'It's as if he's there somewhere in the back of the auditorium,' says John Heley.

The obvious difficulty for anyone moving from chamber orchestra *konzertmeister* to conductor is the change in repertoire. As we have seen, Neville has not always felt completely at home with orchestral music of the late 19th century. What worked at chamber level did not work with symphonies of that period. 'Once you get beyond Schubert, If you try to clarify too much of the

How many does it take to make a BBC lm? John Amis (facing away, foreground) interviews Neville on a canal in Bruges

texture you tend to get too many bones and not enough flesh.'[8] He used a telling metaphor to explain the difficulty he had with the music of Brahms in achieving the subtle shadings required in the orchestra while still keeping the contrapuntal lines clear: 'I wanted to see all the trees. And so you lighten the undergrowth. But then you discover all of a sudden that you no longer have a forest.'[9]

Marriner's talent is to get the music to express itself through the players, rather than trying to impose a personal interpretation on it. The music is made to speak for itself. Having established – from a basis of meticulous preparation – a consensus about how a piece should go, he gives the players plenty of room to tell the story in performance – to add, on the night, the emotional elements, the theatre and the drama.

He has sometimes been accused of failing sufficiently to explore or bring out the emotion in music. Players say he can seem uncomfortable with raw emotion, so that the music becomes too smooth or 'shiny'. Once, a wind player jumped up while Neville was conducting a moody Romantic piece, to protest at his handling of a particular passage.

Neville indirectly answered this kind of criticism with characteristic candour in an interview he gave in the U.S:

'I shy away from the actual words connected with discussing the spiritual part of music. There are certain things that for an Englishman – at least this English-man – cannot be put into words. We've not been brought up to talk about our emotions, but that doesn't mean you don't feel them. I think that theatricality can be contrived to a certain point, but there has to be something else. It gets rather sterile if it's just a series of tricks. Extreme dynamics or tempi may be audience-winning; however, if they have no musical basis, I think that you would run out of steam pretty quickly.' [10]

On only one occasion that I know of has Neville confessed to being emo-tionally overcome while conducting a piece of music: and that was during a performance of Schoenberg's beautiful *Verklärte Nacht* in 1973. 'I really don't know what happened, but that work absolutely destroyed me,' he told an in-terviewer many years later. 'I was deeply upset afterwards in a way that I can't remember ever being before.'[11]

The writer Norman Lebrecht has described chamber orchestra directors like Neville who spread their wings as 'semi-conductors.'[12] Not a flattering word, but intended to differentiate those who have come up the chamber music route, or in some other unconventional way. Neville is seen as a conductor who sparkles in the repertoire which requires the lightness and clarity he is so good at achieving, but is less happy in works which have a brooding or ambiguous intent. This suggests he is best in music that reflects his own character: lively Vivaldi, intense and structural Bach, carefree Handel and genial Haydn, mischievous and lyrical Mozart, mercurial Rossini. He is also well suited to the angularity and precision of modernist works.

It is an attractive theory, but doesn't quite work. For Neville can also produce magnificent Beethoven. Robert Smissen recalls 'spine-tingling moments,' and I myself witnessed a thrilling Beethoven First which he performed at the Musikverein in Vienna. Yet no-one would accuse Neville of sharing Beethoven's temperament. Also, he is very much at home with the arch-romantic Schumann, whose symphonies other conductors can find awkward and oddly scored.

For most of the time, he appears delightfully insouciant, as when during one rehearsal at the Sydney Opera House he told some noisy visitors in the gallery to 'be quiet', without taking the precaution of turning round to see who they were. It was the Queen with her entourage being shown round the building. He is completely at home with young players. I have seen him conduct the 160 teenagers of the National Youth Orchestra in Leonard Bernstein's suite from *West Side Story*. His baton never went more than head high, but the verve and excitement of the playing was a match even for Gustavo Dudamel's high-spirited young Bolivar orchestra. And those who have watched him coaching the National Youth String Academy (started by Roger Garland, a former Academy of St. Martin's violinist, and his wife) have remarked on the intense rapport he has with young musicians.

Chapter Five
FAME AND MISFORTUNE

WE broke off the Academy's story to follow Neville's fortunes as a conductor. With his absences abroad and the arrival of a proper constitution, it could be said that the Academy reached adulthood. Some of the exuberance and high jinks of the early days may have been lost, but the skill and enthusiasm of the players remained undiminished. Through the 1970s and 1980s the band – in its three different guises – enjoyed the sweets of public success, but also the strains of internal discord and a brush with disaster.

The 'big band' forged ahead with a string of symphonic and concerto recordings, culminating in its first, triumphant, film score contract, for *Amadeus*. But the triumph was to have a sorry sequel, when an ambitious project to give the orchestra a proper home in London brought it to the brink of financial ruin.

Meanwhile there were personality clashes inside the chamber orchestra which, in spite of its own run of recording successes, found it difficult to adjust to life without Neville.

For the first ten years of the Academy's life, Neville's wife Molly had done all the administration, unpaid. Working from a table at home, she dealt with agents, promoters, studios and concert halls, booking the players, running the library and keeping the diary. On tour, she became tour manager. At the same time she was bringing up Neville's two children, Susie and Andrew. In 1969 she acquired a helper, Elizabeth Williams, who took over the 'fixing' job, using a card index supplied by Molly which had the players filed in order of preference. Sharing a flat with four other girls, so that the phone was constantly engaged, Liz Williams rigged up an extension for incoming Academy calls from the telephone of a Scandinavian craft shop below. The owner of the shop was unaware of the arrangement, until the musicians, in breach of instructions, began ringing up during the day.

Liz Williams was followed by Christine Johnson. But it was clear that the Academy needed an office. And when Molly began spending months away in the U.S. with Neville, it was decided, in 1972, to advertise for a part-time secretary. The advertisement was answered by Sylvia Holford, 'fixer' for the BBC Symphony Chorus, and herself a trained singer and piano accompanist. Sylvia later became *repetiteur* for Joan Sutherland, travelling to Switzerland to help the diva learn her opera parts. Sylvia gave her directions in the florid passages as if she were driving a car – 'Turn left here, right there…'[1]

The 'office' – minus the box files of music – now moved to Sylvia's flat in Aberdare Gardens in West Hampstead. Sylvia's job quickly became more than secretarial, and full time, and she was re-designated general manager. In this role she saw the Academy through twelve successful years. Katy Jones (then Woolf), who had also trained as a singer and joined the Academy Chorus in 1977, worked with her looking after its engagements.

The new office was not so different from the old. 'I used to do schedules on Sylvia's kitchen table,' Katy remembers. 'And we had a Roneo machine – that skin thing on which you used nail varnish when you made a typing mistake. But we had one of the first answerphones: someone in West Hampstead, an American, came in and fiddled with wires to fix it up, and BT weren't to know. And there was a funny little copying machine which lived in the cupboard.'

At first, all the paperwork fitted into one file. There was no promotion work (in those days it was not necessary) and there was an accountant to keep the books. As the orchestra grew, the workload increased, and Value-Added Tax was introduced – 'an absolute nightmare' according to Sylvia.

The office moved again, to a ground floor and basement in Boundary Road, a few streets away, and new staff came in: Katherine Adams as tour manager, and Hilary Keenlyside as assistant to Sylvia, whom she succeeded in 1985. Hans

Ulrich Schmid, the Academy's new – and increasingly important – German agent, paid tribute to Sylvia's 'mixture of professionalism and enthusiasm which is not too often found in our present musical world.' Katy Jones said: 'She was good fun, Sylvia.'

The elastic band

The Academy could not survive as a concert orchestra – not in London, anyway. With four independent symphony orchestras and a growing collection of chamber orchestras to choose from, audiences rarely filled halls. And since the Academy had eschewed state support from the Arts Council from the start, fearing for its independence, making records and touring in support of them was its real business.

The repertoire of pieces written for a small string band of 16 or 20 players was quickly exhausted and the Academy had to expand to take on bigger works. More players on the books – not just woodwind and brass, but extra strings to balance them – meant more administration, and the 'little band' (as it was called) did not make enough profit to support an expanding office. Even without these constraints, the Academy would probably have grown anyway because of Neville's fear that the players would become bored and stale if they went on repeating the same stuff: as he said, there is a limit to the number of times you can relish playing Vivaldi's *Four Seasons*. After all, did his players not come to the Academy precisely in order to get a break from repetitive symphony work? Then there was Neville's own ambition to record the symphony repertory; and the greatest opportunities in the world for recording were in London. In spite of his absence for much of the year, Neville was on hand to conduct the 'big band' (as the small symphony orchestra was called) in a series of high-profile recordings, culminating with a best-selling soundtrack for the hugely popular film *Amadeus*.

Argo, the faithful label now owned by Decca, could not give the Academy enough work, and its exclusive five-year contract signed with them in 1965 was not renewed, although recordings with them went on until 1983. The Academy was now open to offers, but found its principal partner in Philips, owned by Phonogram, with whom it signed successive contracts right up to 1997. The key figure in this relationship was the producer Erik Smith, who had worked with the Academy in the 1960s when he was at Decca, and who had accompanied Neville to the Pierre Monteux conducting school in 1963.

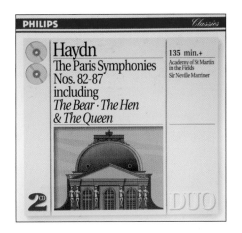

It was Erik's idea to make a series of records with the title 'The Rise of the Symphony' in the style and with the forces employed in the 18th and early 19th centuries, including Johann Christian Bach's *Six Pieces*, Op.3, never before recorded, and Haydn, Mozart and Beethoven. The series was issued as a set of four records in 1971. They were seen as a prelude to recording the entire output of Mozart and Beethoven – including his Ninth, which was reached in 1989, fulfilling the wry prophecy of Stephen Shingles, the viola player, years before that if the Academy ever aspired to play Beethoven's Ninth, he would be off. The Rossini overtures were also tackled, the way having been cleared with his earlier orchestral pieces: the final disc to appear, in 1980, contained obscure titles like *Torvaldo e Dorliska*, *Edipo a Colono*, and *Maometto II*. In all cases Erik and Neville hunted about for manuscripts, or the earliest known editions. The problem of choosing from Haydn's 104 symphonies was solved by selecting the ones with names – *The Surprise, The London* and so on – a neat marketing ploy if not musicologically kosher. Mozart was now seriously revisited, beginning with the compositions he wrote at the age of eight while visiting London with his father in 1764, and orchestrated by Erik to justify his conviction that the young prodigy had intended the sketches as instrumental, not keyboard, pieces. There followed the wind concerti and the rest of the complete cycle of symphonies in editions prepared by Neville, who commented: 'We may in our youth have been a Baroque group, but we've grown up with Mozart.'

Alongside the symphonies was the cycle of piano concertos recorded with Alfred Brendel– one of the closest collaborations the Academy has ever had with a soloist, and resulting in some of the best known of its recordings. If Neville was

Alfred Brendel and Neville Marriner discuss a point during recording of the Mozart piano concertos.

Photo: Mike Evans

apprehensive, he must have been calmed by Brendel's judgment of the project as 'a sort of chamber-music playing… It's not often one finds chamber orchestras of this level of accomplishment,' and his flattering description of Neville as 'an extension of my right arm.' Brendel took six months preparing each piece; both pianist and conductor paid microscopic attention to the scores, and each was played in concert before going into the studio, where two recording sessions were usually enough. The progress of K595 was filmed by Humphrey Burton for London Weekend Television's *Aquarius* programme, and Brendel – who generally hated TV cameras – can be seen mugging so shamelessly that a critic declared him the most accomplished silent comedian since Buster Keaton. The first disc, of K414 and K453, appeared in 1971 and was Critics' Choice in *Gramophone* magazine. The last, completed just before Christmas 1984, contained K175 and K238, and a second double concerto, K242, for which Brendel again chose his former pupil Imogen Cooper. (She had recorded the other, K365, with him in 1977).

Erik Smith and Brendel reconstructed Mozart's piano *Rondo* K382, whose autograph score had been cut into pieces in the 19th century to make greetings cards – only for a complete original to be discovered later in the British Library.

Alongside the symphonic cycles, the Academy was putting out a stream of Baroque and modern music. Thurston Dart achieved a lifetime's musicological ambition when his exotic re-reading of the *Brandenburg Concertos* was brought to the studio in early 1971. Dart himself was seriously ill with cancer, and had to give up playing the harpsichord in the middle of the sessions. He died a few weeks later. The recording became famous – or notorious, with those who did not like Dart's substitution of instruments. Vivaldi was explored in recordings of *L'Estro Armonico, La Stravaganza* and *La Cetra*, the last featuring Iona Brown as soloist-director. These were collected up together with Alan Loveday's *Four Seasons* to make an anniversary box for Vivaldi's 300th birthday in 1978. The Baroque works were prepared mainly by Christopher Hogwood.

Mention should be made of another soloist with whom the Academy worked a good deal at this time. Dame Janet Baker had got to know the band at King's College, Cambridge in the 1960s, and at the Dartington summer school. Now she teamed up with them to record Bach cantatas in 1975, the *Arie Amorose* by Alessandro Scarlatti and various lesser-known Italians in 1978, while appearing in between in two choral works, the *Christmas Oratorio* in 1976 (with Elly Ameling, Robert Tear and Dietrich Fischer-Dieskau under Philip Ledger at King's) and Bach's great *Mass in B Minor* under Neville Marriner the following year. Among modern English composers committed to vinyl were Vaughan Williams, Elgar, Britten, Butterworth and Walton.

During this period, the Academy became, at least for the front desk players, almost a full-time job.

Neil Black, Neville Marriner, Janet Baker and *Tonmeister* Vittorio Negri during recording of the Bach B Minor Mass for Philips in 1977 .

Photo: Mike Evans

The Chamber Ensemble ('The Octet')

We saw in Chapter Three how the Academy grew and mutated in order to expand its repertoire and recording opportunities. The Academy Chamber Ensemble, founded almost by chance in 1967, took some time to get going. Its early tours included the vineyards of Germany and the country houses of Ireland and England. One of them was Levens Hall in the southern Lake District, a Jacobean house famous for its topiary garden and owned by the Bagot family. There were musical connections here. For Robin Bagot was a builder of harpsichords, and the eldest of his three daughters, Priscilla, became the wife of Erik Smith in 1967.

The pace picked up after Malcolm Latchem became the Ensemble's manager in 1977. Before that the repertoire consisted of only half a dozen pieces. Macolm reckons he has played the Mendelssohn Octet, the piece upon which the Ensemble was founded, no fewer than 700 times 'although never quite the same each time.' Under the leadership of Iona Brown, the group began tackling sextets and quintets in order to extend the its range – a practice which continues

The Octet in Smith Square, 1979, before a US tour: L –R Roger Smith, Anthony Jenkins, Roger Garland, Iona Brown, Malcolm Latchem, Stephen Shingles, Andrew McGee, Denis Vigay. One US review carried the headline 'Snow White and the Seven Dwarfs'.

to this day. Its geographical range extended, too, to North America and the Antipodes. Some audiences were extraordinarily loyal. The burghers of Münster in Germany, for example, would host the Ensemble every other year, demand the same programme, and fill the hall each time. The Ensemble's tally of recordings, first under Iona and later Kenneth Sillito, rose to more than 40.

At first The Octet would appear in the same concert with the chamber orchestra. Later, when booked on its own, it was occasionally met by a puzzled promoter demanding 'Where's the orchestra?' Neville Marriner was never entirely convinced that the Ensemble was a good idea. The players did well out of it – the individual fee was about double what they earned playing with the orchestra – but the Academy did not get much benefit. Neville always suspected that it provided a cheap alternative for parsimonious promoters, and so deprived the Academy of work. 'I argued that we were flying the flag in places that could not afford more,' Malcolm said. 'We went to places the orchestra could not go. And if sometimes we went to the bigger venues it was usually in the same year as the Academy.' Stephen Orton, his successor as Octet manager, makes the same defence; he takes care that the group does not queer the Academy's pitch.

The Chorus

Another product was added to the Academy brand in 1974. The Academy Chorus developed out of a proposal by Hans Ulrich Schmid to profit from Germany's enthusiasm for English choirs by taking Bach's *Mass in B Minor* on tour. None of the choirs approached, however, were ready to send a contingent small enough to match the small forces of the orchestra – it was all or none. So Sylvia suggested the Academy find the singers for itself. She knew where to start looking: before joining she had worked both as singer and accompanist for the choral conductor Laszlo Heltay, who now was appointed director. A former pupil of Kodaly's, Laszlo had left Hungary after the Soviet invasion of 1956, entered Oxford University as a postgraduate to read musicology, and formed two choirs there.

The search for singers – the Academy needed 72 for Germany – was thus made easier. Former undergraduates and others who had sung for Heltay at Oxford or later for his Brighton Festival Chorus, stepped forward. Among the assorted doctors, lawyers and other professionals were Robert Key, the future MP for Salisbury (and later a member of the Academy Board); Oz Clarke, who was to give up music for wine-writing; and Katy Jones .

Laszlo Heltay
Photo: Jim Four

One of the singers was recruited after what must count as the shortest musical audition in history. Gerald Finley, a student with a friend in the chorus, came to Sylvia Holford's front door for a try-out. She opened the door. He said: 'Hello!' She said: 'You're in!'. The sound of that one word from him was enough for her.[2] Nor was she mistaken. The young bass-baritone was to become one of the hottest properties on the international opera circuit.

Like most English choirs, the singers were amateurs or students. This was a deliberate decision, because Neville and Laszlo wanted part-timers, and voices that were not 'produced', would blend well, and were light, young and agile to suit the playing style of the orchestra. Vibrato was out. The singers were expected, however, to be good sight-readers: rehearsal time was never going to be generous.

To get the same type of sound from chorus and orchestra, Laszlo copied into his singers' parts the marks that Neville had made in the players', and then rehearsed them to a piano accompaniment. When it came to full rehearsals, the fusion of voices and instruments was underlined by Neville's habit of talking to the singers as if they *were* instruments: he would address the tenors as 'violas', the altos as 'second fiddles' and tell the choir to 'sing this note off the string'. The chorus found it difficult to get used to the peculiar imagery he used for getting what he wanted from them, such as: 'Bring in the washing – it's flapping about.' And they were offended by his habit, acquired when conducting the much less skillful Dartington summer school choir, of giving each section their note just before entry.

In spite of – or perhaps because of – this friction, the 1975 German tour was a resounding success. The critics were divided on Neville's unfamiliar treatment of Bach: some objected to his fast tempi and pronounced articulation; others praised the way he had brought singers and instruments so closely into line that it was hard to tell sometimes which was which. An eminent critic of the *Frankfurter Allgemeine Zeitung* welcomed 'an important new step'. The German audiences loved it, at one concert even rushing the stage. And the recording made for Philips two years later in 1977 stands as a reminder of what a breakthrough this was in the performance of Bach's choral music.

On the tours to Germany and Spain which became regular events, the Chorus had a high old time, as choirs tend to do, with Laszlo the life and soul of the party. His singers found him inspirational, and were happy to turn up after work for a three-hour rehearsal. The players agreed that Heltay had done a brilliant job, creating a chorus to match any in Britain. Some, however, protested that the Academy had no business performing choral works, complaining that tours with the Chorus were too much of a travelling circus. Relations were strained when the Chorus began to demand more of a say in programming, and a Board of its own.

But the public loved the recordings. The first, of Handel's *Messiah* made for Argo, sold a quarter of a million in the first three years. The soloists were Elly Ameling, Anna Reynolds, Philip Langridge and Gwynne Howell, with John Wilbraham, trumpet, Kenneth Heath, cello, Christopher Hogwood, organ,

[continued on page 112]

The last Governor of Hong Kong, Chris Patten with Sir Neville Marriner, 1997.

The Chorus

[continued from page 109] and Nicholas Kraemer, harpsichord. Neville's intention was to do for Handel's oratorio what he had already done for Bach's Mass, and make a decisive break with the ponderous massed-choir treatments of the Victorian age. Again, some critics thought he had gone too far. Geoffrey Crankshaw regretfully gave it the thumbs down, explaining later that the *Messiah* was 'a Rembrandtian score and a Rembrandtian view of God and man, and I think it was treated as a rococo diversion.'[3]

The Chorus went on to make some 30 more recordings up to the mid 1990s, among them, in 1990, Paco Pena's exotic *Misa Flamenca*. In public it appeared with the orchestra at the ceremony for the return of Hong Kong to China in 1997, performed in the theatre at Epidauros, Greece, and at the former World Trade Center in New York. But over the following years opportunities dwindled and the Chorus fell into limbo. It was not formally disbanded, but lay in abeyance, though hopes of a revival lingered.

Iona's reign

Neville's absences in the U.S. made it imperative to find another director for the chamber orchestra. A number of distinguished violinists had stood in, among them Hugh Maguire, Manoug Parikian, and György Pauk, but the old guard on the front desks, found it hard to adapt to their different styles. Accustomed to having everything strictly laid down, they lacked flexibility – or so one of them says now. During the orchestra's second world tour, to Australia and the Far East in 1974, Neville had to go off to his seasonal job in Los Angeles, and left the band in the hands of Malcolm Latchem, principal second violin and a senior member. Malcolm was puzzled by the choice, although he had some experience of leading at the Philharmonia, found it a strain, and after some months asked the Board to find someone else.

One of the obvious candidates was Iona Brown, who had played with the Academy since 1964, had often taken solo parts, and had led for Neville when he was conducting. She had directed briefly in 1972. He considered her the epitome of an Academy player – 'a gifted soloist, a responsive ensemble player, and an opinionated musician.'

But at this moment she was not with the orchestra, having left after some minor altercation; and Carmel Kaine, another possible contender, had taken her place on the front desk. Malcolm now suggested to the Board that he ask Iona to

return, and duly called on her at her home in Salisbury. Iona came back in 1975, and so began a musically successful but somewhat difficult career as Neville's successor in the 'little band'. The job entailed also leading the the Octet, where one of the players described her influence as 'fantastic'. In the chamber orchestra Iona maintained the musical discipline that Neville had created, while more openly expressing the musical feeling.

But Iona, too had ambitions to be an international freelance, and in 1979, after a particularly good tour with the Octet (the waggish headline of one American review was: 'Snow White and the Seven Dwarfs'), she asked to give up that part of her job because it was getting in the way of her parallel solo career. (Another version is that she was eased out of the Octet.) The Board decided to offer the Octet job to Kenneth Sillito, leader of the Gabrieli Quartet, who, as we have seen, Neville had already tried to recruit at a transport café on the A1. This time Kenneth was intercepted at Heathrow Airport, and this time he agreed.

Meanwhile, however, some of the players were getting restive under Iona's command, and a number of them left. The Academy Board decided in 1980 to relieve Iona of her job altogether and let the newly-enlisted Ken take over as musical director. But the letter they sent Iona was ignored, and no-one, it seems was willing to follow it up and confront her. Just as well, perhaps, because – embarrassingly for the Board – it turned out that Ken was in any case too busy with the Gabrieli to take over entirely, and Iona was 're-employed'. She forgave Neville for the incident, but not – or so they felt – the other player-directors involved.

The leadership struggle continued, and Neville tried to clear things up with a letter to Iona in 1985. He proposed that Ken should take over the Octet entirely, and that she and Ken should share the direction of the chamber orchestra. Both were to lead the symphony orchestra which Neville continued to conduct. But Iona would not agree to this latter suggestion, so Ken Sillito, reluctantly at first, had to do it all himself. Ken had up to then very little experience of the symphonic repertoire, and Neville was for ever after grateful to him for taking it on.

[continued on page 118]

Iona Brown

Iona Brown was the daughter of musicians. Her mother was a violinist with the Bournemouth Symphony Orchestra, her father a music teacher and church organist. She was the eldest of four musical children, all of whom became professionals. Timothy was a chorister in the Salisbury Cathedral choir, and principal horn of the BBC Symphony Orchestra and of the Academy. Ian became a conductor and pianist, principally with the Nash Ensemble, and Sally, the youngest, followed her mother into the Bournemouth orchestra as a viola player.

Their father Antony revered Bach, an influence he transmitted to his children. He was also, as it happens, a close friend of William Golding, the Nobel laureate writer: both taught at Bishop Wordsworth's School in Salisbury.

Iona in turn revered her father, even if the relationship could be a stormy one. Her strong will and boundless energy were harnessed not just to making the best music possible. She seemed to need more than that, to win approval, to validate herself, perhaps because she felt – rightly or wrongly – that her father's approval was not unconditional.

In her teens she took lessons from Hugh Maguire, another Academy regular, later playing in his Cremona Quartet. She also studied in Rome with Principe, in Vienna with Odnoposov and with Carlo Van Neste in Brussels, before joining the Philharmonia in 1963 under Otto Klemperer, and the Academy of St Martin in the Fields in 1967. She became a regular soloist at the Proms .

In 1981, encouraged by the cellist Mstislav Rostropovich, who in 1975 had recorded Haydn cello concertos with her, Iona became music director of the Norwegian Chamber Orchestra. Here, in the view of colleagues who worked with her there,

Iona at the NCO and Mariss Jansons at the Oslo Philharmonic between them made a huge impact on the musical life of Norway. Pauls Ezergailis, colleague both in Norway and at the Academy, said of her: 'She was a meticulous perfectionist, very disciplined, but always played with amazing expressiveness. She was inspirational. Hers were some of the most memorable concerts I have ever played.' In 1987, she became director of the Los Angeles Chamber Orchestra, following Neville Marriner and Gerard Schwarz.

During the next few years rheumatoid arthritis in her wrists began to trouble her. She could not reach so far up the fingerboard, which restricted the number of pieces she could perform. The day came when after playing a favourite piece, Vaughan Williams's *The Lark Ascending*, on tour in Japan in 1997, she realised she would never play it again and wrote a postcard home to say so. In 1999 she sold her beloved Stradivarius violin (made in 1716 and known as the 'Booth'), which by a happy coincidence reappeared soon after in the hands of Julia Fischer. For most of her life Iona played a Guadagnini, borrowed from a private individual and bequeathed to the Royal Academy of Music.

Iona Brown:
'a glamorous
spectacle in her
concert dress'

Iona turned increasingly to conducting. She performed a good deal, but found the transition less easy than Neville had done. She had already been guest director of the City of Birmingham Symphony from 1985-9, at the invitation of Simon Rattle. Now she found engagements with the London Philharmonic, Royal Liverpool Philharmonic, Bournemouth Symphony, the Danish Philharmonic and Tokyo Philharmonic. She was not so readily employed by the Academy's 'big band', her last date with them being a Christmas concert in 1999. Her last concert as a conductor was with the LPO in May, 2002, in Salisbury Cathedral on the day she was diagnosed with the cancer which led to her death two years later at the early age of 63. At her funeral in Bowerchalke, the organ music was all Bach and one of the readings was from Golding's *The Spire*.

Iona befriended the great cellist Jacqueline du Pré, whose life and playing career were also cut short (in her case by multiple sclerosis) supporting her in her illness.

Iona earned plenty of public recognition, and was awarded the OBE in the 1986 New Year's Honours list. One of the many tributes written after her death came from Denis Vigay, the veteran cellist who had found Iona particularly difficult to work with but recognised her great ability. She was, he said: 'a violin diva of striking platform presence,' continuing with this picture of her in a gusty evening performance in the ancient Herodes Atticus theatre under the Acropolis:

'I have vivid memories of Iona's swaying figure playing in dark cathedrals or windy amphitheatres, either partially obscured by candle smoke and surrounded by squeaking bats, or with her hair streaming out in the wind, but simultaneously playing The Four Seasons *memorably and beautifully. In chamber music she could produce a pianissimo line and phrasing of magical serenity.'*

Iona's friend and supporter Jo Cole, the Academy cellist who also occupies a senior post at the Royal Northern College of Music, recalled being taken at the age of eleven to hear Iona directing the Academy in Bedford: 'I was instantly captivated by the power visibly emanating from this small lady... whose eyes reminded me of Elizabeth Taylor as Cleopatra and who made a sound on the violin that I adored,' she wrote. 'For me to play in the Academy, directed by Iona, was the happy realization of a childhood dream.'

The great Rostropovich said her playing remained for him 'a brilliant memory of the most exquisite passion and commitment.'

Iona Brown in Osaka

[continued from page 113]

The dual command did not work at all well. The chamber orchestra became almost two separate bands – one consisting of players Iona liked on her team, and the other of those she did not, who played for Ken. In 1985, there was a shakeout of the cello section. The newcomers Stephen Orton and John Heley, both former students of William Pleith (who taught Jacqueline du Pré), also found working with Iona difficult, with the result that she chose a variety of others. Another cellist recruited at this time was Martin Loveday (no relation to Alan), a very fine player whom we met in Chapter One.

All this clouded Iona's relationship with the Academy (though never, it seems, with Neville himself) so that when she had to give up the violin because of the onset of a crippling arthritis, they were reluctant to allow her to stay on as a conductor (which she had also become) or as artistic director. And when she died of cancer, still only 63 years old, her friends felt she did not get from the Academy the recognition she was due.

Friend and foe alike agreed that Iona was a superb musician, passionate and committed to the highest standards. Her brother Tim said she brought a new intensity to the Academy. 'She was quite uncompromising when it came to music. For dynamic contrast, she made me and everybody else play at the limits of quietness. The result was amazing.' Another Academy insider agreed that Iona was sometimes wrong. 'But when she got it right, she was fantastic. Like Neville, she was not always cautious.' Her recordings for the Academy of the Schubert Octet and of Mozart's Oboe Quartet, Clarinet Quintet and Horn Quintet won awards.

Few people outside the Academy knew about the discord within. The public loved Iona's performances. She had terrific stage presence, the ability to communicate her passion for music, and made a glamorous spectacle with her concert dresses. She was, in other words, exactly what audiences thought a talented female musician should look like. Her popular appeal may have added to the resentment felt by some of her colleagues, that they were adjuncts to the projection of her own star quality.

Her temperament may have upset others, but it did not seem to impede her. There might have been a row during rehearsals, perhaps even tears, and her colleagues would wonder how that evening's concert could possibly work. But Iona would come out and give a tremendous performance. It was almost as if she needed the stimulus of an emotional scene to charge her up for the night.

The judgment of one Academy insider is typical. 'Iona was impossible,' she said, 'but worth every minute.'

Having lived for years somewhat in the shadow of Iona Brown, Kenneth Sillito now had a free rein. Hitherto, he had only been able to do the concerts and tours with the chamber orchestra that Iona rejected – which meant the Asian circuit, because Iona disliked flying and long tours. Ken sought to increase the repertoire that the Academy could play without the need for conducting, which he himself had no intention of doing. But he found it hard to get promoters to go along with him. When he offered the *Serenade* by Josef Suk, Dvořák's son-in-law, for a tour in the U.S., he was turned down. 'They probably thought it was by some modern Korean composer,' he said. The merest mention of Shostakovich, Schoenberg, Stravinsky or Bartok had promoters gasping. One way round this was to play the game of the 'innocent ear': a concert audience would hear a piece without being told the composer's name and after the interval would be invited to guess it.[4] *Verklärte Nacht* was a good one to do this with, because while the music is lyrically seductive, the name of Schoenberg is enough to make most audiences run a mile.

Office politics

The period of the triumvirate exposed a serious weakness – the lack of a managerial set up that could sort out personnel problems. Under a new constitution in place by 1984, two companies were created: the Academy Concerts Society, a charitable trust whose Council of Management comprised seven or eight people; and ASM (Orchestra) Ltd., its commercial subsidiary, with a Board consisting of seven player-directors which employed the office staff.

But the real power lay in the hands of Neville. He was chairman of both Boards (at least until later), he chose the player-directors and he co-opted the members of the Council. To him usually fell the job of hiring and firing musicians. That was for several reasons: he had always been recognized as the boss, he was naturally decisive, and the trustees were at that time not businessmen but music-loving friends and patrons.

Neville's loyal supporter, the hard-nosed Californian philanthropist Richard Colburn, used to tell him to choose his Board on 'the principle of the Three Gs'. By that he did not mean the Great, the Good and the Glamorous but, more starkly, 'Give, Get, or Get off!'. In other words, trustees should give money, raise money, or quit. Dick Colburn was himself on the Board for a while. But when he recruited one of his business friends, there were grumbles. 'He was very critical of everything,' said a player director. 'He even complained that the notepaper was too expensive.'

Orchestras are famously difficult to run. Management gurus may see them as models of corporate synergy, a paradigm of goal-orientated self-direction under the guiding hand of the boss (see Chapter Two). But when it comes to their own internal management, it must be said they have little to teach the world.

Whether player-governed like the LSO, or more conventionally structured, there is always tension between the musical side and the money side, between artistic strategy and commercial strategy. The same tension is found outside the arts, even in enterprises like car manufacturing, where engineers are often at loggerheads with the marketing department. It is a familiar problem – or was until the accountants won the contest – in newspapers, where the editorial department is at war with the advertising department. In charitable organisations, where trustees are part-time volunteers – in this case music enthusiasts – the tensions are slightly different, but the gap can be just as wide. Some degree of friction is unavoidable; the only solution is for each party – governors, managers and musicians – to be clear who is responsible for what. That can take time. It took Clive Gillinson, the cellist-turned-manager of the LSO, for example, ten years to get demarcation lines agreed between the all-player Board and the orchestra's management.

One long-time player director of the Academy described his job as an unpleasant responsibility. The Board was too weak, he said, spending hours in meetings without coming to conclusions. The meetings with the trustees were 'miserable'. If it was decided to let a player go, the player directors had the job of breaking the news to someone who was a personal friend, and then had to face the shocked, outraged and sometimes litigious reaction. The fact that Neville had often to act as executioner as well as judge made it no easier.

The structural problem was to be addressed in 2001, with a new constitution merging the two boards into one. How much that helped to reduce the tension between the music and the money we shall see in the next chapter.

Given what has been said, it is no surprise to learn that the job of an orchestra's general manager, squeezed between the needs of the players and the needs of the business, can be very insecure. Some football managers have greater job security - and much larger salaries. Once the office was put on a professional footing, the survival chances of chief executives narrowed alarmingly: After Sylvia Holford, the average tenure was less than five years .

The triumph of *Amadeus*

Things may have been difficult behind the scenes, but in the world outside the Academy was reaching a zenith of musical success, summarised by the one word *Amadeus*. The film of Peter Shaffer's hit play of the same name brought the public flocking. A moving and intriguing – if not exactly historical – gothic fantasy about the young scallywag musical genius whose career was shadowed and early death engineered by Salieri, the jealous elder rival, it introduced a whole new generation to the music of Wolfgang Amadeus Mozart. Indeed, it created a new audience for him. Mozart joined Madonna in the pop charts, which had the classical music pundits asking whether this was a fluke or the beginning of a trend – a 'freak accident or a hopeful omen,' as one put it.

Peter Shaffer was on hand to write the screenplay. But who was to look after the music?

Saul Zaentz, the Hollywood producer of films such as *One Flew Over the Cuckoo's Nest*, and Milos Forman the Czech director asked four advisers to write down the names of the best three interpreters of Mozart in the world. The name of Neville Marriner, at that time still with the Minnesota Orchestra, was the only one to appear on all four lists (some say it was top of all four lists). Neville's reputation for Mozart derived, of course, from the many recordings he and the Academy had made with Erik Smith for Philips in the 1970s. Neville himself believes the decisive influence was Isaac Stern, with whom he had worked in the U.S., and that Stern told Peter Shaffer to use the Academy for the soundtrack of the film.

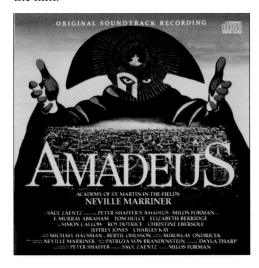

Whatever the sequence, a meeting was arranged with Zaentz, Forman and Shaffer at JFK airport in New York where Neville was changing planes for Minneapolis. Later the trio flew to England and travelled down to the Marriners' country place in Devon to select the music.

There were to be about 50 minutes of music (the play contained just eight). 'I made only one stipulation,' says Neville, 'that it had to be played the way I wanted it played, and not a Hollywood hash-up.' That was agreed, and recording began at Abbey Road in North London just before Christmas in 1982, with Erik Smith in charge.

Most unusually, Neville was given the freedom to choose his soloists – all the singing and playing was dubbed. Among them were Felicity Lott, Willard White, Anne Howells and John Tomlinson. Chorus singers came from the Royal Opera House, the Ambrosian Opera Chorus, the Westminster Abbey choristers under Simon Preston, and of course the Academy Chorus under Laszlo Heltay. Piano solos were played by Imogen Cooper, Ivan Moravec, Christian Zacharias and Anne Queffelec; among other instrumentalists were William Bennett (flute) and Osian Ellis (harp).

But there had been one actor who wanted to sing his own part. Simon Callow, playing the impresario Shikaneder and Papageno in excerpts from The *Magic Flute*, put his hand up and was given time to practise the famous duet with his love-bird Papagena. Sadly for him, the competition was too hot, and the part was dubbed by the Marriners' friend, Brian Kay of The King's Singers, with his wife Gillian Fisher providing the voice of Papagena.

Again unusually, most of the musical soundtrack was recorded before shooting of the film began – a reversal of the usual practice – because in this movie the music was not incidental; it was integral to the story. 'You couldn't cut the music to fit the film,' said Neville. 'You had to make the film around the music.'

Work continued through 1983, with some of the pieces being re-done that November, and a final synchronisation session took place in April 1984.

A poster was produced to advertise the film. It showed a picture of Neville beside one of Mozart, and bore this legend: 'Only two people were qualified to conduct the score of Milos Forman's *Amadeus*. One was unavailable.'

The LP and CD sets of the film score were the best-selling records that Neville and the Academy ever made, and earned everybody – the conductor, the individual players and the company – gratifying amounts of money. 'Everyone got cheques. That was the wonderful thing,' said Katy Jones. 'Even I got cheques, because I sang in it!' A second disc, *More Amadeus,* with some pieces re-recorded, came out in 1985.

The fee for the film score was £50,000. On top were royalties divided between the four principals – Shaffer, Zaentz, Forman and Marriner. Neville said he would like to share his percentage with the orchestra, so they agreed on 2.5 per cent out of Neville's quarter share. 'Then the others did the same, so the Academy got 10

Only two people were qualified to conduct the score of Milos Forman's "Amadeus."

Wolfgang Amadeus Mozart   *Neville Marriner*

One was unavailable.

September 10, in a benefit premiere, hear Marriner and The Academy of St. Martin-in-the-Fields perform Mozart the way Mozart performed Mozart.
Amadeus, the motion picture.
A special preview benefit for the Minnesota Orchestra at the Cooper Theatre

per cent in the end – though I'm not sure they realized what they were doing,' Neville joked. Royalty receipts for the Academy amounted to nearly £200,000 over the first couple of years.

With all that money in the bank and the orchestra's name riding high from Hollywood to Hong Kong, it was not surprising that someone should have come up with a brilliant idea for spending it.

Drowning at Wapping

It was the new general manager Hilary Keenlyside who came up with the brilliant idea. A bright and ambitious young woman who had worked for Scottish Opera, she noted that the Academy had about £80,000 of savings in the Abbey National building society, and thought it should be put to good use. Katy Jones told her that what the Academy needed most was a permanent place to rehearse. Having grown too big for the Marriners' flat, the orchestra had moved to the British Institute of Recorded Sound premises in Exhibition Road, but were now also using churches and halls all over London.

[continued on page 128]

Kenneth Sillito, the miner's son, pictured with his Guadagnini violin atop the Sydney Opera House in October, 1983 for the *Sydney Morning Herald*. The original caption was – of course – 'Fiddler on the Roof'. Ken said the experience was more like 'coalmining in reverse'.

Photo: Sydney Morning Herald

Kenneth Sillito

The story of Kenneth Sillito's musical career has a fairytale beginning, and features a fairy godmother, too. The man who was to become leader of a famous string quartet and director of the Academy of St. Martin in the Fields was born in 1939, the son of a coal miner at Ashington on the Northumberland coast. His father had wanted to be a violinist, but – as was usual in those days – found himself going down the pit at the age of 14. Ken remembers the mining community tucked away in beautiful countryside near the sea. Lorryloads of dark-skinned men would drive past – not miners coming off their shift, but Italian prisoners of war (the 'Eyeties') being ferried to work in the fields.

On Sunday afternoons, father and son used to go for walks along the river near Sheepwash, outside the town, and catch minnows in jam jars beneath the walls of a castle. Ken remembers looking up at the walls and wondering what they concealed. 'That's Bothal Castle,' his father told him. The castle was to play an important part in the little boy's life.

The sound of the violin came to him in the cradle: it was the one thing on the radio (the 'wireless' in those days) which was guaranteed to stop him crying. At the age of seven he was presented with a choice of three instruments, a harmonium, an 'English' concertina, and what he remembers as 'a really rough full-sized violin'. He didn't like the harmonium, and couldn't lift the concertina. So his father set about teaching him to get a sound from the open string of the violin, with the promise of a decent half-size instrument when he could find one.

'It took him about three months. Then he came in one day with it and I came home for lunch – the school was just across the road – and there was the fiddle. He insisted I had to learn it properly – an hour's practice a day, and also half an hour at lunchtime and more at the weekends. I went to a local man, a greengrocer, who knew a bit more about the violin literature and got me going.'

The first live concert he heard was at Newcastle City Hall: the soloist was the young Isaac Stern. 'Even then, I thought, Well, this is not the sort of thing you usually hear!'

Ken used to blame his mother when she called him in off the street to practise, as directed by his Dad. Most boys in those days followed their fathers down the mine, although a few broke away by excelling at sport or science. One of Ken's team-mates in the school football side was a boy called Bobby Charlton. Another friend became a top physicist.

The crucial moment in his life was when, at the age of nine, Ken was heard playing at a local festival by a woman called Valentine Orde. A cellist, teacher and patron of music, Miss Orde pronounced that the boy needed a proper teacher, and sent him to Hermann McLeod in Jesmond. Meanwhile, she co-opted young Ken for Sunday afternoon chamber music sessions at her home. Home turned out to be the keep of the castle at Bothal below which Ken had caught minnows as a small boy.

'So - lo and behold! - I found myself at the age of nine being driven through the gates in the local bank manager's car – he played the viola, after a fashion. We did Haydn quartets, Mozart quartets. I remember especially spring time when the room was full of sweet peas. Now when I smell sweet peas it all comes back. This wonderful lady really fostered me. She gave me not just music, but poetry, architecture, all sorts of artistic things.'

By now probably the best violinist in the county of Northumberland, Ken went to Bedlington Grammar School where the head, 'a mad keen viola player', asked him to play solo in front of the visiting music inspector, another viola player called Bernard Shore. Ken later heard from his parents that he had won a scholarship to the Royal Academy of Music. (They had previously turned down an invitation for him to study in San Francisco).

So, at 14, the age at which his father had gone down the pit, Kenneth moved to London to study at the RAM, continuing the rest of his education at Marylebone Grammar School. Although music schools taught their students as if they were destined to become soloists, Ken knew from early on that he wanted to play chamber music.

At 17 he was at the Dartington summer music school taking lessons from Symon Goldberg, who asked him to play second violin in a Mozart quintet. The contact opened door for him, and Ken soon found himself invited to play at the Aldeburgh Festival under Benjamin Britten. The following year he was leading the Northern Sinfonia. (His association with Aldeburgh and Britten continued for many years, and he now lives not far from the town.)

Called up for national service – one of the last generation to be conscripted – Ken went into the Life Guards, a cavalry regiment which boasted an orchestra for use at banquets and investitures. 'I didn't have to ride. I didn't get near a horse,' he said. 'It was a very cushy number. I used to check in at Windsor barracks to see if there were any duties, then go back to studying. We were made to learn the bugle – you wouldn't believe how long it took – so that we could do guard duty and play Reveille at 5.30 on a frosty morning.'

At 21 the young violinist won a travelling scholarship and chose to go to Rome to study under Remy Principe for a year. He was invited to join the English Chamber Orchestra as associate leader, later becoming principal leader. He formed the Gabrieli Quartet in 1967 and led that for the next 20 years. In 1973 the ECO became very busy 'when a young lad called Daniel Barenboim came along'; the quartet was also busy, and Ken had to make a choice. He chose the Gabrieli. In 1980 he was headhunted to succeed Iona Brown as leader of the Academy Octet. Seven years later when Iona Brown went to California, he gave up the Gabrieli to become sole director of the Academy chamber orchestra.

[continued from-
page 123]
The band needed a home, a base in London, not only for rehearsals but perhaps even for recording. St Martin's church was too busy a place for rehearsals,
there was still nowhere to park, and despite the Academy's connection, it played
there only rarely, usually for anniversaries and other commemorative occasions.

'A great orchestra needs a home,' wrote Ernest Fleischmann, general manager
of the LSO, in 1964. 'It needs regular acoustic conditions to develop its own style
and sound, its personality. Its members should not be required to rush from one
end of London to another… How can even great conductors realise an orchestra's potential, particularly in regard to quality and balance of sound, when every
one of four rehearsals for a concert takes place in a different hall? How can an
orchestra really build up its audience…?'[5]

In the mid 1980s the Government was belatedly attempting to redevelop the
docks of London's East End, ravaged by German bombing during the Blitz in
World War II, and now made redundant by the invention of cargo containers
carried by huge vessels whose draught was too great for the inner docks and so
berthed further downriver at Tilbury.

Through the London Docklands Development Corporation (LDDC), Hilary
learned of a large vacant building in the Shadwell Basin at Wapping, standing
right opposite the riverside pub known to all Londoners and most visitors: the
Prospect of Whitby. The Wapping pumping station was one of five that provided
hydraulic power not only for dockside cranes and bridges such as Tower Bridge,
but for the rotating stages of the London Palladium and Coliseum theatres, and
the lifts of five-storey mansions in Kensington and Mayfair. Fed by coal, its steam
boilers worked pumping engines that helped push – at the peak in the 1930s –
some 33 million gallons of water through 186 miles of pipes under the streets of
the city. Built in 1892, of red brick, converted from steam to electric in the 1950s,
and now Grade II listed, the Wapping station closed in 1977. It was the last in
London – and in the world.

Katy Jones remembers it well:

'It was the most fantastic building. Though people have awful memories now of
Wapping it was the most wonderful building, a fabulous building: full of pigeon
shit and full of machines, a huge area with a sort of gallery, a bit of a basement, all
absolutely appalling and stinking. Neville went in one day and sort of clapped a
bit and decreed the acoustics were wonderful.'

Her enthusiasm was shared by the musicians, who were invited to come and see for themselves. A riverboat stocked with drinks and snacks was chartered to carry the orchestra from Charing Cross pier downstream to the *Prospect*, where they landed, were shown over the site and repaired to the pub for more pints.

The idea was to convert the building to provide not only a rehearsal space for the orchestra, but an office, lockers and lavatories for the players, and a kitchen for making tea. Conduits were to be laid in which recording companies could run their cables. When in the middle of 1986 the development corporation said it was ready to give the orchestra the building and the site, and throw in £250,000 towards the cost of development, imaginations were fired.

Now Hilary and her team saw Wapping as 'a music centre…a superb and exciting opportunity, unique in the world.'

Not only rehearsals and recordings, but films and broadcasts could be made from there, and concerts given for invited audiences (the licensing laws would not permit ticketed performances). Tourists in Trafalgar Square who dropped into St Martin's church asking for the Academy would be directed down to Wapping where they could watch the players at work through a one-way mirror in the foyer. They would find a restaurant, shop and museum. Land could be acquired for an underground car park, above which *al fresco* concerts might be given on summer nights. There would be benefits for the local community, too: perhaps

Inside the Wapping pumphouse in 1987, the view from the East.

Photo: National Monuments Record

a Shadwell festival, and workshops for children. A second chamber orchestra might be formed for local events.

A target date of Spring, 1988 was set for the grand opening, to feature an inaugural concert and the screening of a Channel 4 documentary about the project that was to be made in time for the big night. A commemorative disc – perhaps the first of a series of Academy own-label recordings – and a book were also mooted.

The unfolding vision was further reinforced by an approach from the South Bank Centre, which in April 1986 had taken over the Festival Hall and other venues from the defunct Greater London Council. It offered the Academy a South Bank residency from the autumn of 1987. A river bus could convey the players upstream from their rehearsals at Wapping to their concerts on the South Bank.

At a stroke, the nomadic Academy found itself being offered not one home in London, but two. A public announcement and press conference at the Festival Hall were scheduled for 23rd September, 1986.

As for the funding, that seemed within reach. A feasibility study by accountants Peat, Marwick projected a total budget of £1.5m. of which the Academy would put up £400,000, comprising its royalties from *Amadeus*, sale of the office in Boundary Road, accumulated profits, receipts from an American tour, and profits from the coming season. The accountants suggested income from the pumping station would comfortably exceed running costs: Hilary Keenlyside thought that an overstatement, but that it would be sufficient. Fundraising was to begin with a gala dinner in the Guildhall, followed by similar events in major U.S. cities. More staff were taken on, and the computer system upgraded

Engaged to carry out the conversion was the leading contractor Ove Arup, with its associate Arup Acoustics, which had worked on the Maltings at Snape, near Aldeburgh, on the Henry Wood Hall (the former Trinity Church in Southwark), and the Sydney Opera House. In July, 1986, their estimate for building a rehearsal and recording space was a bit larger than expected: £2.64m. A fine model was made of the 'music centre', at a cost of about £40,000. But this was all manageable. By this time more than £1m had been promised towards an overall target of £5.4m, the office was hoping to raise £2m from American companies and £1.4m from British firms. The Academy felt ready to take out a mortgage of up to £750,000. A minor snag was that the relationship between the charitable body (the Concerts Society) and the trading company (the orchestra) was still a little unclear.

The plan was unveiled on 8th January, 1987, and received a lot of attention in the national press. Pictures appeared of Neville and Iona at the pumping station. Work was to begin in April, but the building estimate had risen, and the opening date was moved to the autumn of the following year.

Over the next two years, impressive dispositions were made in preparation for the big event. But the cost of the project kept rising, and the start date kept receding.

A complicated new management structure was created, with two trading subsidiaries reporting to the main Board. Hilary was executive director, supervising three other directors (finance, development and marketing), each with their own staff, a chairman's committee, and the orchestral administrator and five staff. The office expanded exponentially.

The Board itself was beefed up. In early 1987 the Prince of Wales became a patron of the Society, and in 1988 Baron (Charles) Williams of Elvel, a Labour life peer, a prominent City banker who had played cricket for Essex, was made chairman. An American foundation,with its own executive director, was set up; its Board included Richard Colburn and the *Amadeus* producer Saul Zaentz. In the UK new trustees with financial influence were brought in. Artistic advisers were appointed: Peter Shaffer, Alfred Brendel and Sir Georg Solti.

A fundraiser had been appointed, but more was being spent than was being raised. And it became apparent that the trading company – the orchestra – was being asked to meet bills incurred on behalf of the charitable body, the Academy Concerts Society, which was supposed to be handling the project. Impressed by Hilary's confidence, enthusiasm and undoubted flair, the Boards seemed for a long time unaware of danger. But one person, at least, was alarmed. Hilary's assistant Katy Jones, who was keeping the books and knew the figures, felt she had to say something. Katy attended Board meetings to take the minutes, and in February 1988, she spoke up. This upset relations in the office, and Katy had to leave. She continued working from home, however, as the orchestra's part-time 'fixer'.

In July 1988, funding was arranged with ANZ merchant bank. The Academy had three to five years in which to raise the money. But negotations with the London Docklands Development Corporation were going slowly, and the start of building operations was postponed again, to 1989.

Things rumbled on for several months until, in September, Peat Marwick raised a question. The Academy's charitable status meant that the main Board could not underwrite or subsidise the activities of the orchestra, the trading subsidiary. The situation had to be cleared with the Charity Commission and the Revenue. This was important, because it affected the price at which the orchestra could lease its new home from the parent Society. In November the finance director warned the chairman's committee of this issue.

Now the player directors became alarmed about the escalating cost and the risk facing the orchestra. They were given reassurance. But Neville, Hilary and other members of the Society Board who were financially liable felt it prudent to take out personal indemnity insurance of £1m each. Both the chairman and one of the longer-serving directors, were worried. One was a member of the House of Lords, the other an MP, and neither could afford to be associated with a bankruptcy, or with a charity whose status was threatened.

Another Board member, Lois Sieff, came to the rescue. Mrs Sieff, an American and formerly an actress, was married to Edward Sieff of the well-known Marks & Spencer family; she was an experienced fund-raiser and sat on the Boards of the Royal Court Theatre and the National Theatre. Now she intervened with the Charity Commissioners to prevent them taking any drastic step. For if the Society's entanglement with its trading arm led to the Academy's charitable status being revoked, then all would be lost.

In November Ove Arup told the management that because of inflation and rising interest rates the cost of the conversion, last estimated at £3.8m, was likely to work out at £6.4m. And shortly afterwards the Docklands Development Corporation warned that if it did not very soon get the Academy's assurance that it was going ahead, another occupant for the pumping station would be found.

At about this time Monya Gilbert, Hilary's assistant, also became alarmed, and after reading one weekend a management handbook she had bought at W.H. Smith confided her fears to Molly.

In April, 1989, Peat Marwick began reviewing the project. Meanwhile, Neville visited the pumping station with acoustic engineers from Philips, the recording company, who told him that the place was not large enough for recording symphony orchestras. This was a blow, because letting the hall to other orchestras was to be one of the means of defraying running costs.

A crisis meeting of the Academy Concerts Society was held on 18th September. Peat Marwick's review suggested the Academy had bitten off more than it could chew. Wapping could be salvaged, but only by mounting another appeal for funds, committing the orchestra's future income, and scaling the project down or making it a joint venture with others. The Society's own solvency was questioned, and at one point it was suggested that if the worst came to the worst, the orchestra itself could be sold.

Reluctant to see all the energy and expense wasted, the Board decided to give the project another few months, during which economies would be made, targets for the appeal would be set, revenue would be scrutinised and new investors sought. A joint meeting of the ACS and orchestra Boards was called for Thursday, 28th September.

On the Thursday evening, directors and staff met to discuss details of the Peat Marwick report It became clear that the Academy's financial position was just not viable. The orchestra was not prepared to to mortgage its future, let alone sell itself to new owners. After long hours, it was decided to overturn the previous ACS Board decision, and wind the project down.

It was nearly three o'clock in the morning, and the dream of Wapping was dead.

The Wapping pumping station transformed into an upmarket restaurant and picture gallery.

Chapter Six
A CHANGE OF DIRECTION

Mopping up after Wapping

WITH its 30th anniversary only weeks away, the Academy had been saved. The directors hastened to pick up the pieces. The orchestra's offices had moved to Raine Street, off Wapping lane, to be near the pumping station. Now the former office in Boundary Road was sold for £120,000, wiping out the overdraft. Richard Colburn guaranteed a £200,000 loan and several directors, including Neville, chipped in large sums.[1] Contracts were re-negotiated, some concerts cancelled, and belts were tightened all round. The debacle resulted in the loss of two Board members, the chief executive Hilary Keenlyside – who left with a financial settlement – and several other members of staff. But the orchestra remained viable.

Monya Gilbert was appointed to succeed as chief executive. The daughter of a famous flautist, Geoffrey Winzer Gilbert (one of whose students was James Galway), Monya had trained as a violinist and had adopted her father's middle name in her earlier career playing in theatres, cabaret and on Cunard cruise liners such as the QE2. A colleague described her as having 'an archetypal English charm, and a great sense of humour.'

As for the pumping station, it was swept up in a process of gentrification as waterfront warehouses were converted into apartments for young City bankers and denizens of the Canary Wharf financial megalopolis. The pumping engines are still there, squatting like primitive totems in the main hall and providing modish décor for what is now an upmarket restaurant and exhibition centre.

Although the players breathed a deep sigh of relief, the loss of Wapping was a huge disappointment, regretted to this day. For it left the Academy still without a London home. And as the decade advanced, the need for a base was to become an issue once more.

Great though the internal ructions had been, the public was blissfully unaware of them. Neville and his orchestra – whose workload had doubled in the previous five years – continued to thrive on the reputation gained from the worldwide success of *Amadeus*. In 1988 there was a world tour, taking in Germany, Russia, Japan and the U.S. At home, the Academy for several years performed at the South Bank summer festival, although even with distinguished soloists the concerts were rarely profitable. It was invited to a Mozart week in Salzburg in early 1989, and the following year performed Mozart's *Requiem* at Carnegie Hall to mark the impending anniversary of the composer's death. The Academy fielded its largest-ever orchestra, of 87 players, for a series of concerts under Neville in 1991 which began at the Festival Hall with Anne-Sophie Mutter playing the Brahms violin concerto, and then travelled with her, Paul Crossley and Radu Lupu to Belgium, Germany, Austria, Spain and Portugal. Spain heard the first complete performance of Paco Pena's *Misa Flamenca* when the Academy Chorus under Laszlo Heltay opened the Seville Expo '92 at the city's great cathedral. The Chorus was at Neville's 70th birthday concert at the Festival Hall in 1994 when he conducted pieces starring Alfred Brendel, his own son Andrew and soprano Sylvia McNair. (For this birthday, fellow director Bryan Montgomery gave Neville a 'music table' – a small dining table with six retractable music stands disguised as drawers – and six chairs to go round it).

In 1992, three years after Wapping, Neville took a further step back by giving up the chairmanship of the orchestra Board. He was succeeded by Malcolm Latchem, who did the job for two years before handing over to John Heley. In theory this put more distance between Neville and the band; in reality, the association remained as strong as ever in the public mind, and Neville's appearances with the 'big band' were as frequent as before.

The market slumps

But now another kind of challenge was emerging, one beyond the power of the Academy or any other orchestra to influence. The classical record industry was heading for a deep and lasting slump.

The band had enjoyed a 35-year-long bull market in recording. Founded a few years after the hi-fi craze and the introduction of stereo records, Marriner's Academy and von Karajan's Berlin Philharmonic were the two biggest beneficiaries of the golden age of the LP. A second boom began with the arrival of the compact disc in 1983. Record companies pumped out releases and re-releases for enthusiasts who wanted to buy their favourite records all over again in the new format. 'There was a lot of over-recording,' says James Jolly, editor-in-chief of *Gramophone*, 'and many records which should never have been made.' As a result, the public suffered an acute attack of collective indigestion. The market was saturated, and the companies slammed on the brakes.

For the Academy, whose fame and fortune had been largely built on recording, this was a serious shock. In the second half of the 1990s the work was supplied as much by German companies like Hänssler and Capriccio (which had often recorded Neville with the Suttgart Radio Orchestra) as by Philips or the new arrival Chandos. In the years running up to the 50th anniversary, there were releases of Bach keyboad concertos and other works with Murray Perahia; Brahms and Stravinsky concertos with Hilary Hahn, Bruch with Pamela Frank, a debut album for the soprano Kate Royal, Bach violin concertos with Julia Fischer and, in 2009, compositions by Gordon Getty.

There was no easy way out. Giving concerts in London had never been profitable, even for the chamber orchestra and even at the prestigious South Bank, a fact which was driven home by the Wapping crisis. The band's UK presence as a live group was (with the exception of the Ensemble) negligible. Much depended on sponsors. With the big band Neville had no problem filling halls on tour: he was getting 90 per cent houses. But neither he, nor any other principal conductor of a London orchestra could fill the Festival Hall or the Barbican Centre on their own. The conductorless Academy chamber band, famous as its name was on three continents, did not have the market pull to make concerts viable.

There was only one answer: more overseas touring.

The looming squeeze had been foreseen. The orchestra acquired a new manager in 1995, when Monya Gilbert moved to the U.S. She was Rowena ('George') Brown, who had worked for the London Philharmonic Orchestra and was described as 'a good, solid, sensible businesswoman.' The management consultants Booz Allen & Hamilton were commissioned to review the Academy's prospects and come up with ideas that would help see it safely into the new millennium.

In summary, the consultants noted the Academy's high reputation and musical excellence, but called for an artistic 'vision' and a sense of direction. Could the band continue as both a chamber and a symphony orchestra? What new kinds of musical 'event' could it lay on? Who was to devise the strategy and how should it be carried out? Here the consultants were pointing to the essential confusion of roles between ACS, the charitable society, and ASM, the orchestra, and – even more important – raising the question who (or what combination of persons) would replace Neville as figurehead and artistic overseer.

The new general manager was worried. She told the Board that a 'painful discussion' needed to take place about artistic quality. She pointed to the competition from other bands, and the ageing of audiences for classical music; the Academy had to get 'sharper, less dusty,' and become so attractive that players and conductors queued up to work with it. It might prove impossible, she said, to maintain a first-class orchestra which kept changing size. Above all, she worried about what would happen after Neville Marriner retired. She saw that the relationship with him was unique – 'the orchestra's greatest strength, but also its future weakness.' These questions were to become ever more urgent, as we shall see.

The Board decided not to change the three formats: the Ensemble, the chamber orchestra and the small symphony orchestra, expanding only when Neville wanted to conduct. As for repertoire, the 'artistic roots' of Baroque and early classical would be redefined, allowing further incursions into 20th century music.

An important innovation was that the chamber band would now tour with celebrity soloists. In some ways, this was a return to the earlier days of the Academy, when it consisted of 16-20 players performing the string repertoire. The difference was that in those days solo parts were taken by members of the band: now they were performed by international celebrities.

Unofficial but regular partnerships were forged with leading musicians of the day, including the young conductor Daniel Harding and the violinists Gil Shaham, Pamela Frank, Janine Jansen and Anthony Marwood. The latter made his soloist-director debut with the Academy in 2002 with *Distant Light*, a concerto by the Latvian composer Peteris Vasks, reflecting his interest in contemporary works. His later tour as actor-soloist in Stravinsky's *The Soldier's Tale* with seven Academy players (and sponsored by Carol Colburn Høgel, Richard Colburn's daughter) was hailed as a particular success, a model of the new kind of musical 'event' that was needed to engage young audiences.

The strongest partnerships were with Joshua Bell, Julian Rachlin and Julia Fischer. Joshua Bell knew the band from his 1986 recording of the Mendelssohn and Bruch concertos. He began to take it on tour: first to his homeland of the U.S., later to Germany, Spain and Central Europe, with occasional concerts in London. Players described him as a brilliant director who did not take a long time in rehearsal because he knew what he wanted. 'He doesn't say much but persuades you with the way he plays,' said one. They admired his ability to get dazzling renditions of big pieces such as Beethoven's *Symphony No. 7* or his *Coriolan Overture* from the front desk.

Julian Rachlin, the Viennese violinist – who also performs on the viola – was another whom the Academy found sympathetic, quite apart from his wonderful playing, especially of the Romantic repertoire. The admiration was reciprocal. Rachlin told me he had followed the band avidly since childhood, buying many of its records. As for Julia Fischer, whose attachment to the Academy began when she was still in her teens, we saw in Chapter One what an impact she made on players and audiences and how determined she was to make room for the Academy in her increasingly busy schedule.

A most significant appointment was made in 2000 when, following an initial approach from John Heley, Murray Perahia became principal guest conductor. Perahia, who had won the Leeds Piano Competition in 1972 as a sublime player of Mozart, was no stranger either. He had recorded the two Mendelssohn piano concertos with Neville in 1974 and performed the five Beethoven concertos with him at the Festival Hall in 1988. Now he would be directing from the keyboard or conducting from the front. For all his musicality, Perahia did not pretend to be a great conductor. What he brought – apart from his wonderful playing – were new ideas about musical architecture, identifying moments in the score which were crucial to the overall narrative, which players found inspirational.

Under George Brown, there was a managerial revolution. Although Neville had taken at least two steps back – the first when he pursued his own career as a conductor after 1969, the second when he gave up his chairmanship of the orchestra Board in 1992 – his presence was still deeply felt and highly influential. His advice was sought; he still had a say in hiring and firing, and in choice of repertoire; and his long personal contact with players was maintained through

'Dazzling renditions':
Joshua Bell, the American
violinist.

the 'big band'. John Heley, while chairman of the ASM (Orchestra) Board, had opened things up by making sure, for instance, that players were told if their future with the band was under discussion. Now George Brown and others proposed to go further – to make the players become self-governing, like other London-based symphony and chamber orchestras. But self-governance, for a charity-owned orchestra, turned out to be a non-starter.

Instead, the Academy's constitution was changed to simplify the structure and to give the players more power within it. In 2001, the trading company ASM (the orchestra) became a holding company, responsible only for financial transactions. Control was vested in a unitary Board of the Academy Concerts Society (ACS), the charitable trust, whose seven (later eight) directors would include two (later three) players and would be elected by the players. Neville left the ACS Board. Now his only official connection with the Academy was as its 'Life President', a title he already held.

The 60-plus players who formerly constituted a pool of 'regular casuals' became, along with the non-executives, Members of the Academy. This meant extra security and some rights: they could vote at annual general meetings. There were still no contracts – the Academy remained a part-time orchestra of freelance musicians – and therefore no *right* to play. But advance concert schedules were

Murray Perahia, who became principal guest conductor in 2000, bringing 'new ideas about musical architecture'.

Photo: Jim Four

sent out and members had the right of first refusal. They were less likely in future to be jettisoned because of one bad performance.

George Brown had intended to stay to see these important reforms through, but her circumstances changed and she could not fulfil that hope. She left in 2000 and was replaced by John Manger, a man of charm who seemed to attend every concert and to know every musician in London. But his reign proved short. He left in 2004, and was replaced from inside the organisation by Dawn Day, his assistant, who had been recruited by George Brown in 1997 from the London Philharmonic, where she was concerts manager. Dawn was not made chief executive, but general manager reporting on an almost daily basis to the new chairman of the Board.

The new chairman, Trevor Moross, was joint managing director of a Knightsbridge property company. He had come originally from South Africa, and joined the ACS Board in 2001. Business-like, enthusiastic and committed, he took a close interest in the running of the orchestra, though his was a non-executive, unpaid job.

Thus the Academy entered the millennium with a new structure and a change of life dictated by market forces. In all three formats the players were now to spend most of their time for the Academy on the road. That put more strain on families, especially the younger ones – although the drawbacks of touring were familiar enough by now.

The pattern was as follows for the three groups. The 'big band's' only regular appearances at home were at the 'Mostly Mozart' summer concerts at the Barbican under a variety of conductors – and these were discontinued after 2008. Thanks to the dedication of Hans Ulrich Schmid (and latterly of his daughter Cornelia) in Germany, Neville was taking the 'big band' down the Rhine each

New Year, with final concerts in Berlin or Vienna. There were a few engagements further afield. The 'little band' toured widely in Europe, more regularly in the U.S. and occasionally in Asia. Only the Ensemble had a regular programme of UK concerts, with American and other overseas touring in addition. As already noted, circumstances were squeezing the band back into its old shape – 20-plus string players and winds – but with solos now 'contracted out' to international stars.

This pattern meant that the office could not afford to employ more than about four people. Diminishing engagements for the 'big band' – which earned the big money – meant funds were short for promoting concerts, and for employing full-time fundraising, marketing and public relations people. The absence of London concerts made fundraising difficult. The office ticked over mainly on the surplus from the big European and American tours and from small grants from trusts and foundations, with sporadic help from generous individuals.

The Academy owed its increasing dependence on American and German audiences not only to the energy of its agents, but also to the loyalty of classical radio stations in both countries which continued to broadcast its records and keep the names of Marriner and the Academy in front of the public. These audiences were pleased to discover that the Academy's musicians displayed in the flesh the same fire and focus as they conveyed on record. The presence of big-name soloists was obviously a draw, too – and whether the Academy could prosper without them was one of the questions awaiting a definitive answer.

This reliance on the 'living legacy' of the records was made clear to me on a snowbound January evening at the *Philharmonie* concert hall in Berlin. All but 200 of the hall's 2,400 seats had been sold at up to €90 each for a concert by the 'big band' under Neville – and that in spite of the rival attraction of Daniel Barenboim with his West-Eastern Divan Orchestra performing at the city's *Konzerthaus* the same night.

In random conversations before the concert I learned that most people had heard the Academy but few had seen it. One couple said their latest Academy recording was now ten years old, but they had read a league table of world orchestras which rated the Academy second to the Dresden *Staatskapelle* and in front of the Berlin Philharmonic – in whose hall we were now standing. (A magnificent new hall, I should add, whose design – an irregular polyhedron with blocks of seats angled in different directions to mask the great size of the auditorium – has been copied elsewhere). A woman who had come as one of a party said she had many records and found *der Klang* (the sound) very special. Another admirer of *der Klang* had come all the way from Frankfurt. A young couple with 'lots of records' said they had come to see Sir Neville for the first time. And a retired technical engineer from Bosch-Siemens told me that it was his first time, too. 'I have a radio in every room in the house, and one in the car, where I listen to *Kulturradio* [a Berlin classical music channel]. 'I can't explain why I like the orchestra so much. I haven't got the right words for it,' he added. 'But I have heard Neville Marriner so often I feel I know him.'

The Academy's transition from recording orchestra to touring orchestra seemed to have worked. In an article about Neville's 80th birthday, Norman Lebrecht added his endorsement: 'The record legacy was successful, but it was the live Academy that altered the ecology of concert life, reviving the chamber ensemble as a viable alternative to big bands, and forcing orchestras everywhere to improve string intonation.'[2]

As the 50th anniversary approached, and with the diary shrinking, it became obvious that the 'elastic band' which had mutated so successfully over its lifetime to keep step with the market could no longer delay the next evolutionary step. Although not immediatley threatening, the banking crisis of 2008 which precipitated a deep economic recession was a reminder that artistic organizations depending on sponsorship could no longer wait on events but must take the initiative. Another, more relevant factor, was the turmoil inside the record industry caused by a secular change, the digital revolution: who knew what would happen now that music-lovers could download the equivalent of 3,000 albums into an electronic player no bigger than a pack of cards?

In the summer of 2008 the players, led by their two representatives on the Board, Lynda Houghton and Harvey de Souza (later to be joined by Christopher Cowie) began to press for action. Privately, many players recognized that they had allowed things to drift, had become too passive – even complacent – and had failed to take their share of the responsibility left by Neville's official (but certainly not emotional) detachment from his orchestra. Their immediate concern, of course, was the dwindling diary of engagements. There was no unanimity about whether – or if so, how – an attempt should be made to replace the irreplaceable Neville. Some wanted to maintain maximum independence; others accepted that commercial realities made that impossible. But they were pretty unanimous in feeling that when it came to questions of artistic policy – what the orchestra should play, and with whom – they, the players, should be listened

to more closely than hitherto. Among specific questions to be answered were: What was to happen to the 'big band'? Should they find a home in London? What was the relationship with St Martin's church?

As a result, nearly 20 years after management consultants first raised the questions, and eight years after they were raised again by George Brown, there was a sense that things were at last moving forward. New people were about to come onto the Board, (including two former Academy players) a new general manager was being sought, and intensive discussions between players and directors were beginning.

But no more powerful impetus could be imagined than that which was about to come from the founding director, the father of the Academy family, the 84-year-old Sir Neville Marriner.

Neville puts the question

It was January, 2009, and we were at the Musikverein, Vienna's jewelled casket of a concert hall and the world's high temple of classical music. Outside, a rare snowfall had transformed the city into a Pissarro painting, with intersecting tramlines etched into the grey-blanketed boulevards circling the Schwarzenbergplatz. Inside we were warmed by the golden radiance of Theophil Hansen's late 19th century Grecian fantasy: its Ionic columns, paintings of Apollo and the Muses, and its two rows of gold-plated caryatids gazing impassively into the auditorium, arms folded over naked breasts.[3]

Musicians love this hall. Built before acoustics became a science, it happens to have a perfect resonance, a lucky by-product of the architect's neo-classical taste. Because of the hall's rectangular shape the concert platform is relatively narrow, which suits a small symphony orchestra. The strings find it easy to play absolutely together, while the winds can blow their heads off in the tolerant acoustic. According to engineers who travel to Vienna to study this marvel, the elements which break up the space – the coffered ceiling, the balconies and even the pensive caryatids lining the walls – provide 'an ideal spread of sound waves.' The raised wooden floor of the hall, and its suspended wooden ceiling act as sounding boards, rather like that of a piano, or a violin.[4]

From a seat in the stalls circle, positioned just behind the cellos, I was watching the last rehearsal of a ten-day tour which had taken the 'big band' through Germany to Berlin, on to Budapest, and thence to Vienna. Neville was on the podium, dressed in a favourite shirt of red, blue, green and yellow stripes over a white polo-neck, taking the 46 players through the programme in his calm, unhurried way, his small gestures elaborating the detail, adding the emphases, making space for solo passages. In Beethoven's *Symphony No. 1*, he was unhappy with the opening two chords, *pizzicato* strings and woodwind in a cadence which usually marks the end, not the beginning of a piece. ('Beethoven's fault', he said later. 'He was still learning.') In Mendelssohn's 'Italian' symphony, he stopped to have a go at the horns about the length of a quaver (although they seemed to be playing immaculately). The clarity of the slow movements, with every note ending as cleanly as it began, was soothing, the energy of the fast movements exhilarating like being driven in a sports car you know will never come off the road.

There was an extraordinary camaraderie about this session. The players seemed to be enjoying each other's company, and the music. The atmosphere was almost festive, an end-of-term, end-of-tour feeling, no doubt enhanced by the sensation of playing in the fabulous Musikverein auditorium in their 50th anniversary year. What came next was more striking still. As the last notes died away, Neville lowered his baton, folded his arms, and spoke.

He thanked the orchestra – 'all of you, every one' – for the high standard of their playing during the tour. He congratulated them on a making 'a good noise – as good as it has ever been in 50 years'. 'It's none of my business anymore,' he continued, 'but I find it incomprehensible that we have to wait three months before we meet again when your name is known everywhere.' He then urged the players – all of them, not just the front-desk stalwarts – to get involved in putting that right.

It was a short speech, but Neville's remarks to the orchestra that wintry January afternoon in Vienna were unprecedented. Few of the players, including veterans, had ever heard him speak in quite such a way before. They were very moved, some to the point of tears.

That evening, the orchestra came out to a packed house, and played as if possessed. After the encores, Neville went round shaking the hands of all the front desk players. It had been a special sort of night. A Viennese dowager sitting in the stalls circle inclined towards her neighbour and said: 'I've been coming to this theatre for 60 years and I've seen every famous orchestra in the world. But I've never heard a concert better than that.'

After the traditional end-of-tour drinks party, Neville invited my wife and me to join him and Molly for dinner at the Hotel Imperial. As usual after a concert, he talked of other things, reminiscing about Los Angeles and their exotic neighbours at the Colburn compound, and the giant swimming pool, 'the biggest in Beverly Hills.' Yet he kept coming back to the Academy, wistfully observing that he could no longer – or should no longer – try to take matters into his own hands.

With those remarks in the Musikverein, Neville had not only made plain his own feelings but had said out loud what many others already felt. Intentionally or not, he had also alluded to the big question: could the Academy of St Martin in the Fields survive its founder-director, and live another 50 years?

There was nothing wrong with the musical machine: the Rolls-Royce was in beautiful shape, its engine sounding as good as ever. All that was needed was better navigation and a new road-map. It was they, the players – Neville Marriner's musical family and heirs – who had to help find it.

Sir Neville and Lady Marriner
at home in Devon.
Photo: Jane Bown

FOOTNOTES

CHAPTER 1

1   As it happens, Julia's recording of the *Four Seasons* with the Academy was staged in the great glasshouse of the National Botanic Garden of Wales.

2   *Academy Newsletter*, Spring 1995.

3   I am told that the celebrated Yuri Bashmet got round this by putting his viola case in the hold, and sitting with the viola itself on his knee.

4   Steinhardt, *Violin Dreams*, p. 100

CHAPTER 2

1   When the Orange County reviewer in 2008 complained that he had found a performance under Neville Marriner fine, but dull, and likened the Academy to a Toyota, a reader corrected him: 'at least a Lexus, or a top-end BMW', and reprimanded him for seeing the Academy's technicianship but not its musicianship.

2   *The Strad*, October 1986, p. 389

3   *ibid.* p. 90

4   *Oxford Companion to Music*, Conducting, 7.

5   The phrase used spontaneously by many of the players I have interviewed

6   It was the legendary football manager Bill Shankly, Scottish manager of Liverpool who, when a reporter complained that he was treating an upcoming match as if it was a matter of life and death, replied: 'I can assure you it is much, much more important than that.'

7   Morrison, *Orchestra*

8   The scheme was started by Roger Nierenberg, director of the Jacksonville Symphony Orchestra, Florida, and music director of the Stamford Symphony Orchestra, Connecticut.

9   Barenboim *Everything is Connected*

10   Seth, *An Equal Music*, p. 199

CHAPTER 3

1   Harries, introduction May 1981

2   Harrries, p. 210

3   Churchill's widow Jean thinks it was her husband who first thought up the idea.

4   'The Academy of St Martin-in-the-Fields' by Michael Bowie, *RCM Magazine*, Summer Term 1960

5   Interview in *The Strad* magazine 1986, pp 389-90.

6   The leaders of no fewer than three major orchestras played with the Academy: Hugh Maguire of the BBCSO, Andrew McGee of the LSO and Ronald Thomas of the Bournemouth Symphony.

7   Ian Hampton replaced Wilfred Simenauer and played second cello at this concert. Anthony Howard (violin) and Stanley Mant (cello) played on the Ireland tour.

8   For this and many other details that follow I am indebted to Susie and Meirion Harries.

9   Harries p. 31

10   *ibid,* p. 51

11   *ibid,* p 54

12   *ibid,* p. 69

13   *ibid,* p 92

14   *ibid,* p. 75

15   *ibid,* p. 78-9

16   *ibid,* p. 87

17   In a letter to Neville's daughter Susie (Harries p.116)

18   The Ensemble and the Chorus are described more fully in Chapter Five.

CHAPTER 4

1　The Academy of Ancient Music

2　Speaking to the author.

3　Harries, p. 132.

4　An anecdote about this piece has it that Britten, after conducting the first performance at Coventry Cathedral in 1962, was heard to say as he left.: 'Well, the idea was good.'

5　Neville believes that if re-recordings are omitted, his tally may be the greater.

6　Or perhaps he was thinking of Richard Strauss's advice to young conductors: 'Don't look at the brass – it only encourages them'.

7　Harries, p. 141-2

8　Interview with Dennis Rooney in *The Strad*, Oct.1986, p. 390

9　*ibid.*

10　*Connoisseur's World*, August 1983

11　*The Strad*, October 1986.

12　Lebrecht, *The Maestro Myth*.

CHAPTER 5

1　Katy Jones's recollection

2　*ibid.*

3　Quoted in Harries, p. 191

4　The phrase is from Robert Simpson, BBC producer, composer and musicologist

5　In his submission to Lord Goodman's 1964 inquiry into the future of the London orchestras: see Morrison, p. 195.

CHAPTER 6

1　When Colburn's bank was taken over in 2000, it was discovered that the loan was guaranteed by a company which no longer existed. Colburn, by now 91 years old, paid off half the loan. After his death in 2004, his daughter Carol paid the rest.

2　'The Master Marriner', *Evening Standard*, 5th May, 2004

3　Hansen (1813-1891) was a philhellene Danish architect who had studied and worked for eight years in Athens.

4　More details can be found at the website **www.musikverein.at**

CHRONOLOGY

1726	'New' church of St Martin-in-the-Fields completed
1956	Neville Marriner joins LSO as principal second violin
1958	Academy chamber group formed
	Oct 26. First St Martin's concerts
1959	Academy's first 'professional' concert: Friday, 13th November

1960s

1960	First overseas tour: Ireland.
1961	First record made, 11 string players, with L'Oiseau-Lyre.
1963	NM and Erik Smith at Monteux conducting school
1965	Five-year contract signed with Argo.
1964	First Academy visit to Dartington summer music school
	Iona Brown joins Academy.
1966	'Lift-off' record: Rossini String Sonatas
1967	NM conducts (with bow) Stravinsky's *Apollo and Pulcinella* ballet music.
	Academy Chamber Ensemble ('The Octet') founded.
	First European tours.
1968	Ensemble records Mendelssohn's *Octet* for Argo.
1969	NM goes to US as first director of Los Angeles Chamber Orchestra; leaves LSO
	Vivaldi's *Four Seasons* with Alan Loveday a best-seller

1970s

1970	Contract signed with Philips.
	Last annual Dartington visit.
1971	Academy becomes limited company.
	NM associate conductor of the Northern Sinfonia.
1972	Sylvia Holford becomes office manager.
	Academy's first world tour
1974	Academy Chorus founded
	Second world tour
1975	Iona Brown becomes director of the chamber orchestra.
	Second contract with Philips. NM signs separate conductor's contract.
	German tour with Chorus (Bach *Mass in B Minor*)
1975-8	Academy at London South Bank Summer Music Festival
1979	NM appointed music director of Minnesota Orchestra, Minneapolis
	Time Magazine article
	NM made CBE

1980s

1980	Kenneth Sillito succeeds as director of the Ensemble. Shares direction of the chamber orchestra.
	NM on Desert Island Discs with Roy Plomley.
	First orchestral tour of U.S.
	21st birthday concert at St Martin's church
1981	Harries book published.
1982-4	*Amadeus* film score recorded
1984	Change of constitution: Academy Concerts Society and ASM (Orchestra) Ltd.
	25th anniversary concert at Royal Festival Hall
1985	NM knighted (KBE). Hilary Keenlyside becomes chief executive
1986	Wapping pumping station project begins
	NM leaves Minneapolis
1987	The Prince of Wales become patron for two years
1989	Wapping project called off.
	Academy's 30th anniversary

1990s

1990	Monya Winzer Gilbert succeeds as chief executive
1992	Academy wins Queen's Award for Export Achievement
	Academy performs Paco Pena's *Misa Flamenca* at Seville Expo
	NM leaves orchestra Board
1994	NM's 70th birthday concert at Festival Hall
1995	Rowena ('George') Brown succeeds Monya Gilbert.
	Booz-Allen Hamilton produces strategic plan
1997	NM with Academy in Hong Kong for handover ceremony
1999	Philip Stuart's discography published

2000s

2000	Murray Perahia appointed principal guest conductor
	John Manger succeeds 'George' Brown
2001	New constitution: unitary Board established
2004	Trevor Moross becomes chairman. Dawn Day becomes general manager.
	Death of Iona Brown
2008	Gala concert with Mozart's *Mass in C Minor* for refurbishment of St Martin-in-the-Fields church.
2009	Academy's 50th anniversary.
	NM's 85th birthday; Molly Marriner's 80th.
	NM gets 'lifetime achievement' Grammy award
	Imelda Dervin appointed (interim) general manager.

ACADEMY PLAYERS : 1959 – 2009

Collated by Katy Jones, who writes:

The players listed below have all played their part in the life of the Academy. Some stayed for a while and then went on to pursue solo careers. Some stayed for a short time but made a lasting impression. Some stayed for a long time and provided continuity over the years. Some made regular appearances with the 'big band'. Some played with us for a time, went off to do other things, and then came back to rediscover what they had previously so enjoyed.

The task of listing players from booking sheets spanning fifty years was a mammoth one. I apologize to anyone who doesn't find their name in the line-up. We would love to hear from you.

September 2009

VIOLIN

First appearance in the 1960s: Neville Marriner, Norman Nelson, Trevor Connah, Tessa Robbins, Malcolm Latchem, Tony Howard, Alex Lindsay, Gerald Jarvis, Raymond Keenlyside, Hugh Maguire, Peter Gibbs, Carmel Kaine, Michael de Saulles, Neil Watson, Iona Brown, Diana Cummings, Sydney Castle, Andrew McGee, Ursula Snow, Alan Loveday, John Wakefield, John Willison, Jeffrey Wakefield, Sam Artis, Nigel Murray, Basil Smart, Charmian Gadd, Perry Hart, Jurgen Hess, Sydney Humphreys, Carl Pini, John Brown, Galina Solodchin, Jose Garcia, Sylvia Rosenberg, Peter Thomas, Penny Howard, Ronald Thomas, Roy Gillard, Sidney Mann, Peter Poole, John Knight, Ernest Scott, William Benham, Richard Studt, John Georgiadis, Peter Pople, Colin Staveley, Colin Sauer, Howard Davis, Sheila Nelson, Barry Wilde

First appearance in the 1970s: Tony Howard, Stephen Srawley, Brendan O'Reilly, David Roth, Jeffrey Wakefield, Maurice Brett, Peter Carter, Kelly Isaacs, Nona Liddell, Bela Dekaney, Josef Frohlich, Louis Carus, John Ludlow, Rosemary Ellison, Marilyn Taylor, Richard Deakin, Christopher Hirons, Godfrey Salmon, Michael Freyhan, Marcia Crayford, David Woodcock, John Holloway, Manoug Parikian, Jack Rothstein, Irvine Arditti, Graham Cracknell, Elizabeth Perry, Jonathan Strange, Elizabeth Hunt, David Takeno, Douglas Weiland, Roger Garland, Simon Standage, Ann Hooley, Chris Bevan, Christopher Warren-Green, William Hennessey, Alex Balanescu, Macek Racowski, Paul Barritt, Fiona Vanderspar, Gyorgy Pauk, Louise Williams, Hugh Bean, Barry Griffiths, Susan Lynn

First appearance in the 1980s: Iain Mackinnon, Lynn Fletcher, David Ogden, Andrew Watkinson, Peter Hanson, Kenneth Sillito, Theresa Ward, Joan (Chica) Robertson, Jacqueline Hartley, Jeremy Painter, Nicholas Ward, Elizabeth Edwards, Briony Shaw, Adrian Levine, Sophie Barber, Rita Manning, Miranda Fulleylove, Duncan Riddell, Robert Salter, Jonathan Rees, Gregory Ellis, Jane Carwardine, Keith Pascoe, Robert Heard, Philip Levy, Jonathon Evans-Jones, Thelma Handy, Paul Manley, Thomas Bowes, Patrick Wastnage, Jennifer Godson, David Juritz, Cathy Thompson, Elizabeth Layton, Philippa Ibbotson, Jackie Shave, Peter Manning, Katherine Loynes, Rebecca Hirsch, Susannah Candlin, Pauls Ezergailis, Helen Paterson, Julian Tear, Ian Humphries, Patrick Kiernan, Ralph de Souza, Iris Juda, Sophie Langdon, Ursula Gough, Harriet Davies, Richard Milone, Edmund Coxon, Adrian Levine

First appearance in the 1990s: Jessica O'Leary, Jackie Hartley, Steven Smith, Simon Smith, Robert Atchison, Nicoline Kraamwinkel, Patricia Calnan, Martin Burgess, Eleanor Matthieson, Elspeth Cowey, Enrico Alvares, Douglas Mackie, Miranda Playfair, Harvey de Souza, Elizabeth Suh, Helena Rathbone, Manon Derome, Jan Schmolck, Lucy Gould, Darrell Kok, Edmund Butt, Diane Daly, Amanda Smith, Mark Butler, Clare Hayes, Jeremy Morris, Elizabeth

Williams, Daniel Bell, Christopher George, Matthew Ward, Catherine Morgan, Thomas Elliott, Rebecca Scott

First appearance in the 2000s: Morven Bryce, Kathryn Hunka, Fiona Brett, Mia Cooper, Martin Gwilym-Jones, Alison Dods, Miya Ichinose, Helena Smart, Richard Blayden, Rakhi Singh

VIOLA

First appearance in the 1960s: Maurice Loban, Brian Thomas, Simon Streatfield, Stephen Shingles, Kenneth Essex, Margaret Major, Sylvia Rosenberg, Diana Cummings, Elizabeth Watson, Alec Taylor, John Graham, Graeme Scott, Ian Jewel, John Underwood, Brian Hawkins

First appearance in the 1970s: Keith Lovell, Caroline Sparey, Tony Jenkins, Csaba Erdelyi, Jan Schlapp, Roger Chase, Roger Best, Ludmilla Navratil, Garfield Jackson, Peter Lale, Simon Rawson, Roger Williamson, Donald McVay

First appearance in the 1980s: Catherine Marwood, Levine Andrade, Kathy Burgess, Yuko Inoue, Matthew Souter, Sally Beamish, Tim Grant, Rachel Bolt, Leon King, Andrew Parker, Robert Smissen, Joan St Leon, Rosemary Sanderson, Douglas Paterson, Katie Wilkinson, Bridget Crouch, Edward Vanderspar, Deborah Lander, Nicholas Barr, Timothy Boulton

First appearance in the 1990s: Martin Humbey, Marina Ascherson, Naomi Brown, Fiona Bonds, Steve Tees, Judith Busbridge, Martin Outram, Susan Knight, Catherine Bradshaw, Ian Rathbone, Peter Sulski, Terence Nettle, Esther Geldard, Duncan Ferguson, Riccardo Zwietisch, Rosemary Curtin

CELLO

First appearance in the 1960s: Stanley Mant, Wilfred Simenauer, Kenneth Heath, Denis Vigay, Derek Simpson, Terence Weil, Joy Hall, Elinor Warren, Jennifer Ward Clark, Charles Tunnell, Martin Robinson, Peter Willison, Ross Pople, Michael Evans, Gillian Steele, Alan Dalziel

First appearance in the 1970s: Thomas Igloi, Moray Welsh, David Smith, Roger Smith, Chris van Kampen, Marilyn Sansom, Stephen Orton, Gillian Thoday, Lesley Shrigley-Jones, Alexander Baillie, Benjamin Kennard

First appearance in the 1980s: Lionel Handy, Christine Shillito, Anthony Pleeth, Susan Dorey, Robert Bailey, Andrea Hess, Martin Loveday, Naomi Butterworth, John Heley, Tim Hugh, Sebastian Comberti, Andrew Shulman, Kathy Thulborn, Chris Vanderspar, David Daniels, Simon Morris, Nicki Thomas, Robert Irvine, Jo Cole, William Schofield, Joely Koos, Alastair Blayden

First appearance in the 1990s: Jonathan Tunnell, Jonathan Williams, Amanda Truelove, Nicola Baxter (now Tait)

First appearance in the 2000s: Judith Herbert, Nicholas Cooper, Jane Oliver, Sarah Suckling

DOUBLE-BASS

First appearance in the 1960s: John Gray, Rodney Slatford, Robin McGee, Jeff Clarke, Stuart Knussen, Adrian Beers, Michael Brittain

First appearance in the 1970s: Christopher Laurence, Jack McCormack, John Cooper, Nigel Amherst, Simon Carrington, Keith Marjoram, Peter Hetherington, Philip Sims, Ian Anderson, Barry Guy, Valerie Botwright, John Steer, Tom Martin, Gerald Newson, Duncan McTier, Raymund Koster

First appearance in the 1980s: Keith Woods, Peter Buckoke, Chi-Chi Nwanoku, Lynda Houghton, Stephen Williams, Paul Speirs, Ian Webber, Paul Marrion, Christopher Wescott, Martin Vigay, Paul Sherman, Enno Senft, Stephen Mair, Ian Hall, Anthony Hougham

First appearance in the 1990s: Chris West, Cathy Elliott, Clare Tyack, Roger Linley, Leon Bosch, Diane Clarke

FLUTE/PICCOLO

First appearance in the 1960s: Richard Adeney, William Bennett, James Galway, Peter Lloyd, Norman Knight, Patricia Lyndon

First appearance in the 1970s: Richard Taylor, Edward Beckett, David Butt, Susan Milan, Frank Nolan, Celia Chambers, Kate Lukas, Linda Coffyn, Alan Baker, Henry Messent, Julian Coward

First appearance in the 1980s: Jonathan Snowden, Lenore Smith, Sebastian Bell, Jim Gregory, Philippa Davies, Kate Hill, Christine Messiter, Averill Williams, Adrian Brett, Paul Edmund Davies, Keith Bragg, Sarah Brooke, Martin Parry, Pat Morris

First appearance in the 1990s: Jaime Martin, Michael Cox, Sarah Newbold

First appearance in the 2000s: Andrew Nicholson, Karen Jones, Daniel Pailthorpe, Robert Manasse

OBOE/COR ANGLAIS

First appearance in the 1960s: Peter Graeme, Michael Dobson, Roger Lord, Neil Black, Jimmy Brown, Janet Craxton, Celia Nicklin, Susan Leadbetter, Antony Camden, Geoffrey Wareham

First appearance in the 1970s: Michael Winfield, Tess Miller, Sarah Barrington, Edwin Roxburgh, Maurice Checker, David Theodore, Graham Salter, Barry Davis, Angela Tennick, Andrew Cauthery, Melinda Maxwell

First appearance in the 1980s: David Presly, John Lawley, Gordon Hunt, George Caird, Christine Pendrill, Geoffrey Browne, Julia Girdwood, Katie Clemmow, Christopher O'Neal, John Lawley, Jane Marshall**First appearance in the 1990s:** Christopher Cowie, Rachel Ingleton, Josephine Lively, Lucy Foster

CLARINET/BASS CLARINET/BASSET HORN

First appearance in the 1960s: Ronald Moore, Basil Tschaikov, Richard West, Jack Brymer, Steven Trier

First appearance in the 1970s: Prudence Whittaker, Thea King, Daphne Down, Thomas Kelly, Ronald Moore, Colin Bradbury, Bernard Walton, Michael Harris, Herbert New, Hale Hambleton, Keith Puddy, Gervaise de Peyer, Sidney Fell, Julian Farrell, Antony Pay, John Stenhouse, Roy Jowitt

First appearance in the 1980s: David Campbell, Angela Malsbury, Andrew Marriner, Michael Collins, Joan Enric Lluna, Nicholas Bucknall, Mark Tromans

First appearance in the 2000s: Barnaby Robson, Nicholas Carpenter, Emily Sutcliffe, Thomas Watmough

SAXOPHONE

First appearance in the 1960s: Steven Trier

First appearance in the 1980s: John Harle

BASSOON/CONTRA-BASSOON

First appearance in the 1960s: William Waterhouse, Cecil James, Patrick Milne, Roger Birnstingl

First appearance in the 1970s: Gwidyon Brooke, John Harper, David Rees, Deirdre Dundas Grant, Howard Etherton, Brian Sewell, Martin Gatt, Roger Hagger, Graham Sheen, Felix Warnock, Richard Skinner, David Miles, Ian Cuthill, Wendy Phillips, Neil Levesley, Michael Chapman

First appearance in the 1980s: David Chatterton, Stephen Maw, Gavin McNaughton, Meyrick Alexander, Julie Andrewes, Rachel Gough

First appearance in the 1990s: Robin Kennard

First appearance in the 2000s: John McDouglas

HORN

First appearance in the 1960s: Alan Civil, Timothy Brown, Barry Tuckwell, Martin Shillitoe, Anthony Tunstall, Denis Quaife, Tony Chiddell, Shirley Civil, Nicholas Hill, Dennis Brain, Tony Catterick, Shirley Hopkins

First appearance in the 1970s: Nicholas Busch, Ian Harper, David Gray, Anthony Tunstall, Gordon Carr, Christopher Satterthwaite, Ifor James, Ronald Harris, Ian Beers, Geoffrey Bryant, Julian Baker, Ronald Harris, Colin Horton, Colin Horsley, Denzil Floyd, Neil Sanders, James Beck, Robin Davis, John Pigneguy, Bob McIntosh, Christian Rutherford, Anthony Halstead, Peter Francomb

First appearance in the 1980s: Derek Taylor, Susan Dent, Richard Watkins, Jim Handy, Chris Larkin, Ian Harper, Michael Thompson, Richard Bissill, Jim Rattigan, Frank Lloyd, Tim Jones, Francis Markus, Peter Merry, Simon Rayner

First appearance in the 1990s: Stephen Stirling, Richard Clews, Beth Randell, Mikaela Betts, Michael Murray, Joanne Hensel, Tim Caister

First appearance in the 2000s: Alexia Cammish, Nicholas Hougham, Caroline O'Connell

TRUMPET

First appearance in the 1960s: William Lang, John Wilbraham, Michael Laird, Philip Jones

First appearance in the 1970s: Iaan Wilson, Ian Mackintosh, William Stokes, William Houghton, Crispian Steele-Perkins, John Wallace, Ted Hobart, Jim Watson, Gerald Ruddock, Mark Emney

First appearance in the 1980s: Simon Ferguson, Andrew Hendrie, Mark Bennett

First appearance in the 1990s: Andrew Crowley, Brian Thomson

First appearance in the 2000s: Mark David, Niall Keatley

TROMBONE

First appearance in the 1960s: Denis Wick, Roger Brenner

First appearance in the 1970s: Peter Gane, Frank Matheson, Tom Clough, Eric Crees, Steve Saunders, Peter Harvey, David Purser, Ray Premru, Roger Groves, John Iveson, John Edney

First appearance in the 1980s: Arthur Wilson, David Chandler, Leslie Lake, Roger Harvey, Lindsay Shilling, David Stewart, Christopher Mowat

First appearance in the 1990s: Patrick Jackman, Simon Wills, Dan Jenkins, Amos Miller, Graham Lee

TUBA

First appearance in the 1970s: Ashley Wall

First appearance in the 1980s: Steve Wick, Patrick Harrild, James Gourlay

151

First appearance in the 1990s: Oren Marshall, Martin Knowles

HARPSICHORD/ORGAN

First appearance in the 1960s: George Malcolm, Harold Lester, John Churchill, Philip Ledger, Christopher Hogwood, Simon Preston

First appearance in the 1970s: Andrew Davis, Colin Tilney, Trevor Pinnock, Nicholas Kraemer, Alastair Ross, Erik Smith, Stephen Barlow, Alan Cuckston, John Toll, John Birch

First appearance in the 1980s: Ian Watson, Paul Daniel, John Constable, Andrew Lucas, Ivor Bolton

PIANO

First appearance in the 1970s: Roger Nunn, Clifford Benson, Ian Brown

First appearance in the 1980s: John Alley

HARP

First appearance in the 1960s: Skaila Kanga

First appearance in the 1970s: Nuala Herbert, John Marson

First appearance in the 1980s: Osian Ellis, Isabel Frayling-Cork, Alison Martin

First appearance in the 1990s: Helen Tunstall, Thelma Owen

TIMPANI

First appearance in the 1960s: James Holland, Tristan Fry

First appearance in the 1970s: David Corkhill, Alan Taylor, Ray Northcott, Gary Kettel, Bobby Howes

First appearance in the 1980s: David Stirling, Alan Cumberland, Norman Taylor

First appearance in the 1990s: Ian Wright

First appearance in the 2000s: Martin Gibson

PERCUSSION

First appearance in the 1970s: Ronnie McCrea, Michael Skinner, Peter Greenham, Steve Coltrini, Tim Barry, Harry Smailes, Nigel Shipway, Peter Chrippes, David Johnson, Jack Lees

First appearance in the 1980s: Derek Price, Stan Barratt, Eric Allen, Derek Price

First appearance in the 1990s: Julian Poole

LUTE

First appearance in the 1960s: Robert Spencer

First appearance in the 1980s: Dorothy Linell

RECORDER

First appearance in the 1960s: David Munrow, Philip Pickett, Rachel Beckett

First appearance in the 1980s: Catherine Latham

GAMBA

First appearance in the 1970s: Adam Skeaping, Joseph Skeaping, Denis Nesbitt, Margaret Richards, Oliver Brookes

First appearance in the 1980s: William Hunt, Charles Medlan

ACADEMY OF ST MARTIN IN THE FIELDS MEMBERSHIP AS AT SEPTEMBER 2009

Violin: Kenneth Sillito*, Harvey de Souza*, Martin Burgess*, Jennifer Godson*, Richard Blayden, Fiona Brett, Mark Butler, Pauls Ezergailis, Catherine Morgan, Jeremy Morris, Helen Paterson, Miranda Playfair, Rebecca Scott, Helena Smart, Amanda Smith, Matthew Ward, Elizabeth Williams

Viola: Robert Smissen*, Fiona Bonds*, Duncan Ferguson, Martin Humbey, Ian Rathbone, Nicholas Barr

Cello: Stephen Orton*, John Heley*, Martin Loveday, Susan Dorey, William Schofield, Jo Cole

Double-bass: Lynda Houghton*, Leon Bosch*, Catherine Elliott

Flute: Michael Cox*, Sarah Newbold

Oboe: Christopher Cowie*, Rachel Ingleton

Bassoon: Graham Sheen*, Gavin McNaughton*, Richard Skinner

Horn: Timothy Brown*, Stephen Stirling*, Michael Murray, Susan Dent, Joanne Hensel,

Trumpet: Michael Laird,

Trombone: Roger Harvey*

Timpani: Tristan Fry*,

Harpsichord/piano: John Constable*

* denotes principal

THE STRING OCTET, 2009:

Kenneth Sillito, Harvey de Souza, Martin Burgess, Jennifer Godson, Robert Smissen, Duncan Ferguson, Stephen Orton, John Heley

ACADEMY OF ST MARTIN IN THE FIELDS CHORUS 1975-77

Director: LASZLO HELTAY

compiled by Katy Jones and Sylvia Holford

Sopranos

Rachel Boswell, Barbara Boothman, Kate Brown, Janet Byers, Sybil Chambers, Gill Collymore, Sally Crosher, Catherine Denley, Helen Dixon, Louise Dixon, Heather Dobbin, Rona Eastwood, Carole Ellefsen, Gill Halifax, Jenny Hill, Sylvia Holford, Lucinda Houghton, Margaret Houston, Heide Hughes, Christine James, Helen Jones, Phyllida McCormick, Lindy Marriott, Daphne Middleton, Alison Monk, Sarah Mounsey, Mary Jane Mowat, Christabel Mulvey, Elizabeth Norman, Lorely Powell, Elisabeth Priday, Joan Rivers, Sue Radford, Mary Smith, Vanessa Smith, Alison Stamp, Rae Thomas, Mary Wiegold, Elisabeth Williams, Jane Willmott

Altos

Shirley Beresford, Elisabeth Anne Black, Stella Booth, Eleanor Boulter, Rachel Britton, Tim Brown, Gill Buzzard, Julian Clarkson, Patrick Collin, Philippa Dodds, Penny Feather, Liz Forgan, Maureen Gadd, Jane Glover, Brian Gordon, Mary Hewison, Susannah Howard, Richard Hunt, Mary King, Isabel Nisbet, Katharine Payne, Margaret Peirson, Alan Privett, Katy Roberts, Christopher Royall, Michael Sullivan, Frederick Walker, Julia Williams, Ruth Williams

Tenors

Keith Beck, Peter Birts, Christopher Chivers, Robert Coupe, Christopher Davey, Peter Ellefsen, Philip Fryer, David Gregory, Ben Gunner, Christopher Hand, Robert Key, Andrew King, Arthur Lindley, Alan Maries, Keith Maries, Howard Milner, Charles Metcalfe, John Naylor, Neil Page, John Pearce , Mark Pellew, Richard Pulham, David Roy, Antony Sargent, Donald Storer

Basses

Howard Arman, Robert Asher, Michael Boswell, Alan Brafield, Oz Clarke, Giles Clayton, Graham Cooper, Hugh Davies, Morys Davies, Giles Dawson, John Dexter, Martin Elliott, Douglas Gerwin, Jim Godwin, Christopher Green, Jeremy Hyne, George Kozlowski, Stephen Jackson, Richard Lloyd Morgan, John Myerscough, Tim Pryor, Richard Savage, John Sloboda, John Smyth, Charles Talbot, Chris Tickner, Peter Williams

(apologies for errors or omissions)

SOME NOTABLE ACADEMY and MARRINER RECORDS

With about 600 discs to its credit, the Academy is the world's most recorded chamber orchestra. (The most recorded symphony orchestra is the LSO)

NEVILLE MARRINER'S TOP TEN, 2006

(with date of recording)

Rossini *Barber of Seville*, Philips 1982

Vivaldi *Four Seasons* (Alan Loveday), Argo 1969

Elgar *In the South*, Collins Classics 1990

Richard Strauss *Metamorphosen*, Argo 1969

Brahms *Symphony No 4*, Hännsler 1997

Dvořák *Symphony No 8*, Capriccio 1990

Tchaikovsky *Symphony No 3*, Capriccio 1990

Schoenberg *Verklärte Nacht*, Argo 1969

Stravinsky *Pulcinella Suite*, EMI 1981

Bach Cantatas (Janet Baker), EMI 1975

PHILIP STUART'S TOP FIVE CURRENTLY AVAILABLE (2009)

'English Music for Strings', Double Decca, Penguin Classics

Weill and Vasks violin Concertos (Marwood), Hyperion

Mozart Piano Concertos 20,23 etc.(Brendel), Philips

Rossini Complete Overtures, Philips

Bach Piano Concertos 3,5,6,7, (Perahia), Sony

RECENT ACADEMY RELEASES

(by date of recording)

Getty *Suite, Overture, Three pieces*, etc., Pentatone 2009

Bach *Violin Concertos* (Julia Fischer), Decca 2008

Vivaldi *Four Seasons* (Joshua Bell), Sony 2007

Fauré *Requiem* (The Sixteen, Christophers), Coro 2008

Kate Royal (soprano) debut recital (Gardner), EMI 2007

McCartney *Ecce Cor Meum* (Greenaway), EMI Classics 2006

Haydn *Cello Concertos* (Rostropovich, dir. Iona Brown), 1975, Euroarts DVD

Nicola Benedetti plays MacMillan, Mendelssohn, Mozart, Schubert (MacMillan), DG 2006

Mozart *Donaueschingen Musik* (Academy Ensemble, Blomhert) Pentatone 2006

'The Golden Voice' (Joseph Calleja, tenor) Decca 2005

Giacomo Meyerbeer *L'Esule di Granata* (Carella), Opera Rara 2005

Beethoven *String Quartet* Op. 127 trs. for string orchestra (Perahia), Sony 2003

Mozart *Clarinet Concerto*, Quintet (Andrew Marriner, Sir Neville Marriner), Pentatone Classics, 2004

SELECTION OF ACADEMY RECORDINGS BY INTERNATIONAL RECORD REVIEW, 2004

Bach *Orchestral Suites*, Argo 1970

Bizet *Symphony in C*, Argo 1973

Handel *Concerti Grossi* op. 6, op 8; organ concertos, *Water Music and Firework Music* (Decca)

Vivaldi *L'Estro Armonico, La Cetra*(dir. Iona Brown), *La Stravaganza* (Decca)

Corelli Op. 6 *Concerti Grossi*, 1973-4, (Decca)

Prokofiev *Symphony No 1* 'Classical', Argo 1973

Barber, Copland, Cowell, Creston, Ives, Argo 1975 (Decca)

Dvořák *Serenades*, Philips 1981

Tchaikovsky *Serenade for Strings and Souvenir de Florence*, Argo 1968

Elgar, Vaughan Williams, Butterworth, Warlock et al ('The Essential Music of England') (CD 1997)

Bach *Brandenburg Concertos*, Philips 1980

Bach *Art of Fugue*, Philips 1974

Rodrigo and Guiliani *Guitar Concertos* (Los Romeros), (Philips Duo)

Mozart *Symphonies, Divertimenti, Serenades, Piano Concertos* (Alfred Brendel), (Philips Complete Mozart edn. 1991)

Bach *Harpsichord Concertos* (Igor Kipnis, ASMF as 'The London Strings'1967-70), (Sony)

Beethoven *Symphonies* Nos 1 and 2, Philips 1970.

Schubert *Symphonies*, Philips 1981-4

Bruch *Violin Concerto* No 1/ *Scottish Fantasy* (Akiko Suwanai), Philips 1996

Gounod *Symphony* No 1 and 2, Philips 1997

Schumann *Symphonies* 1-4, Hänssler 1998

NEVILLE MARRINER WITH OTHER ORCHESTRAS

Respighi *Ancient Airs and Dances*, Los Angeles Chamber Orchestra, EMI 1975

Stravinsky *Danses Concertantes*, LACO, EMI 1974

Elgar *Miniatures*, Northern Sinfonia, EMI 1970

Saint-Saëns/Schumann *Cello Concertos* (Lynn Harrell), Cleveland Orchestra, Decca 1981

Haydn/Vieuxtemps *Violin Concertos* (Cho-Liang Lin), Minnesota Orchestra, CBS 1982 (Sony)

Bizet *L'Arlesienne/Carmen suites*, London Symphony Orchestra, Philips 1978

Mendelssohn *Midsummer Night's Dream*, Philharmonia, Philips 1983

Tchaikovsky *Suites* No.3,4, Stuttgart Radio Symphony Orchestra, Capriccio 1987

Haydn *Masses*, Dresden Staatskapelle, EMI 1986

OTHER SELECTIONS:

Beethoven *Eroica* Symphony, Philips 1982

Haydn *Paris Symphonies*, Philips 1981

Mendelssohn *Octet*, Argo 1967

'Rise of the Symphony' 4 discs, Philips 1971 .

'Mozart in Chelsea': from 'London Sketchbook' K15 (arr. E. Smith), Philips 1971

Torroba *Concierto Iberico* (Los Romeros), Philips 1979

Nicholas Maw *Life Studies*, Argo 1978

Bach *Brandenburg Concertos* (ed. Thurston Dart), Philips 1971

Strauss *Metamorphosen*, Argo 1968

Walton *Sonata for String Orchestra*, Argo 1972

THE ACADEMY CHORUS

(from 27 recordings made with the Academy)

Handel *Messiah*, Argo 1976

Bach *B Minor Mass*, Philips 1977

Mozart *Requiem*, Philips 1990*

Haydn *Creation*, Philips 1980

Paco Peña *Misa Flamenca* (dir. Laszlo Heltay), Nimbus 1991

Bach *Magnificat/Vivaldi Gloria*, EMI 1990

OPERAS (all with Philips)

Mozart *Die Entführung* 1978, *Le Nozze di Figaro* 1985, *Cosi fan tutte* 1988-9, *Il Re Pastore* 1989, *Die Zauberflöte* 1989, *Don Giovanni* 1990

FILM SOUNDTRACKS/MUSIC

'*Amadeus*' 1982-4; '*More Amadeus*' 1985

'*The English Patient*', (Gabriel Yared, Harry Rabinowitz) 1996

Walton (arr. C Palmer): '*The Battle of Britain*', '*As You Like It*', '*Hamlet*', '*Henry V*', '*Macbeth*', '*Richard III*'

NEVILLE MARRINER'S DESERT ISLAND DISCS

(interview with Roy Plomley,1980)

The pieces he chose included no Baroque, and no Mozart because, he said, it would have been invidious to choose one performer he had worked with over another. (Janet Baker was the exception):

'Mendelssohn, *Elijah*

Elgar, *Violin Concerto*

Berlioz, *Romeo and Juliet*

'*There is No Rose*' (Choir of King's College, Cambridge)

Ravel, *Schéhérazade* (Janet Baker)

Schumann, *Symphony No 4*

Schoenberg *Verklärte Nacht*

Walton, *Violin Concerto*

In first place, because his son Andrew had been a member of the King's College Choir, he put 'There is No Rose'. The book he chose was Life on Earth *by David Attenborough; and for his 'luxury', his violin.*

SOME AWARDS (1968-2009)

Three Edison Awards (1968-70).

'HiFi News & Record Review' Audio Award to Neville Marriner.

Decca (Holland)'Golden Tulip' award for 12 1/2 years of recording.

'Wiener Flötenuhr' for complete Mozart wind concertos

'Grand Prix de l'Academie Charles Gros' for Mozart early symphonies

'Wiener Flötenuhr' for Mozart piano concertos with Alfred Brendel

NM made Commander of the British Empire

Decca (L'Oiseau-Lyre and Argo) gold disc for over 1m records sold.

Grammy award 'Best Choral Recording' for Haydn's *The Creation*

Thirteen gold discs for soundtrack of film *Amadeus*

Queen's Award for Export Achievement (1993)

Philips' Classic CD award for Gounod Symphonies

'Hestia' award from Sopot, Poland

'Grand Prix du Disque' for Schubert *Octet* (dir. Iona Brown)

'Wiener Flötenuhr' for Mozart *Oboe Quartet*, *Clarinet Quintet*, *Horn Quintet* (dir Iona Brown)

Grammy for Brahms and Stravinsky violin concertos (Hilary Hahn), Sony.

Sir Neville Marriner: Grammy award for lifetime achievement (2009).

* Chosen by *Gramophone* Magazine as best available version

BIBLIOGRAPHY

Barenboim, Daniel, *Everything is Connected: the Power of Music* (London, Weidenfeld, 2008)

Cooke, Deryck, *The Language of Music* (OUP, 1959)

Harries, Meirion and Susie, *The Academy of St Martin in the Fields* (London, Michael Joseph, 1981).

Johnson, Malcolm, *St. Martin-in-the-Fields* (Phillimore & Co, Chichester, 1995)

Lebrecht, Norman, *The Maestro Myth: Great Conductors in Search of Power* (Simon & Schuster, 1991).

Morrison, Richard, *Orchestra: The LSO, a Century of Triumph and Turbulence* (London,, Faber, 2004).

Priestley, J.B., *Trumpets over the Sea: being a rambling and egotistical account of The London Symphony Orchestra's engagement at Daytona Beach, Florida, in July-August, 1967* (London, Heinemann, 1968).

Scholes, Percy A., *The Oxford Companion to Music*, Tenth Edition (OUP, 1983).

Scruton, Roger, *Understanding Music* (Continuum, 2009)

Seth, Vikram, *An Equal Music* (London, Phoenix House, 1999).

Smith, Erik, *Mostly Mozart* (Winchester, Porcellini Publications, 2005)

Steinhardt, Arnold, *Violin Dreams* (Houghton Mifflin 2008)

Stuart, Philip, *Marriner and the Academy: a record partnership* (ASM Orchestra Ltd., 1999)

ILLUSTRATION ACKNOWLEDGEMENTS

Page references

Argo 36
J.&A. Beare 24
Conrad Bjørshol record sleeves
Pavel Antonov 33
Jane Bown 146
Decca 46, 48, 70
Mike Evans 104, 105
Jim Four x, 108, 140
Philippa Garner 79
Julian Hann 66
Kenneth Heath 57
KIPPA 68
Mary Morris 61
Simon Morris 24
Andrew McGee 15, 25
Musica Viva Australia 14
National Monuments Record 129
Charles Rodrigues/Stereo Review 56
Hans Skarrup 84
Star Tribune 88
Sydney Morning Herald 124
Ciaran Tyler Endpapers, xiv, 1, 19, 23, 28, 29, 31, 32, 40, 42, 55, 80, 86, 100, 114, 134, 137, 141
Christian Tyler 3, 34, 39, 49, 50, 92, 144
Reg Wilson 83

INDEX

Page numbers in italic refer to illustrations